IE Business Publishing

IE Publishing | Knowledge and Palgrave Macmillan have launched a collection of high-quality books in the areas of Business and Management, Economics and Finance. This important series is characterized by innovative ideas and theories, entrepreneurial perspectives, academic rigor and practical approaches which will make these books invaluable to the business professional, scholar and student alike. IE University is one of the world's leading institutions that shapes leaders with a global vision, an entrepreneurial mindset and a humanistic approach to drive innovation and change in organizations. Palgrave Macmillan, part of Macmillan Group, has been serving the learning and professional sector for more than 160 years. The series, put together by these eminent international partners, will enable executives, students, management scholars and professionals worldwide to have access to the most valuable information and critical new arguments and theories in the fields of Business and Management, Economics and Finance from the leading experts at IE.

More information about this series at
http://www.palgrave.com/gp/series/14857

Santiago Iñiguez
In an Ideal Business

How the Ideas of 10 Female
Philosophers Bring Value
into the Workplace

Santiago Iñiguez
IE Business School
Madrid, Spain

IE Business Publishing
ISBN 978-3-030-36381-9   ISBN 978-3-030-36379-6 (eBook)
https://doi.org/10.1007/978-3-030-36379-6

© The Editor(s) (if applicable) and The Author(s), under exclusive license to Springer Nature Switzerland AG 2020
This work is subject to copyright. All rights are solely and exclusively licensed by the Publisher, whether the whole or part of the material is concerned, specifically the rights of translation, reprinting, reuse of illustrations, recitation, broadcasting, reproduction on microfilms or in any other physical way, and transmission or information storage and retrieval, electronic adaptation, computer software, or by similar or dissimilar methodology now known or hereafter developed.
The use of general descriptive names, registered names, trademarks, service marks, etc. in this publication does not imply, even in the absence of a specific statement, that such names are exempt from the relevant protective laws and regulations and therefore free for general use.
The publisher, the authors and the editors are safe to assume that the advice and information in this book are believed to be true and accurate at the date of publication. Neither the publisher nor the authors or the editors give a warranty, expressed or implied, with respect to the material contained herein or for any errors or omissions that may have been made. The publisher remains neutral with regard to jurisdictional claims in published maps and institutional affiliations.

This Palgrave Macmillan imprint is published by the registered company Springer Nature Switzerland AG
The registered company address is: Gewerbestrasse 11, 6330 Cham, Switzerland

For Juan Ramón Zamorano Guilló

Acknowledgements

Over the years, there are moments when the different threads of our personal life seemingly entwine, taking on a special meaning. This book is the result of one of these fortunate syntheses, where a sense of purpose, experience, education and desire converge, shedding light on the path taken, as well as producing a certain calm.

My hope is that the female philosophers I have selected for study in this book, along with the businesswomen and entrepreneurs who have kindly agreed to be interviewed, will inspire other women—and men—from the business world. I would like to express my admiration and gratitude for their time, generosity and example.

This is a work that has assembled the thoughts, ideas and lessons of a career, and so the list of acknowledgements is infinite, as is my gratitude to the people I have had the good fortune to work with and to know personally—my friends, colleagues and students.

In the first place, I would like to mention Diego del Alcázar Silvela for his inspiration, his teachings and his support as mentor and friend over the last three decades during which we have worked together. I would also like to thank his son, Diego del Alcázar Benjumea, who has inherited his father's entrepreneurial spirit and passion for education, and with whom I am fortunate to work alongside in mapping the future strategy of IE University.

I could not have written this book, nor found respite, without the support of the superlative leadership team at IE University: Salvador Carmona, Rector; Juan José Güemes, Economic Vice President; Macarena Rosado, Legal Advisor; Gonzalo Garland, Vice President of Development; and Teresa Martín Retortillo, Head of IE Exponential Learning. Similarly, my heartfelt thanks to my comrades at the head of the institution's different schools and units: Martin Boehm, Dean of IE Business School; Martha Thorne, Dean of IE School of Architecture and Design; Javier de Cendra, Dean of IE School of Law; Manuel Muñiz, Dean of IE School of Global and Public Affairs; Lee Newman, Dean of IE School of Human Sciences and Technology; Antonio de Castro, Vice-rector of Alumni; Nick Van Dam, Head of the Center for Learning Innovation; and Marco Giarratana, Vice-rector of Research.

Almost two decades ago, anticipating the approach of the academic institutions in our cluster, we began our research and dissemination activities in the vital areas of diversity and inclusion. Celia de Anca has directed the center that coordinates these initiatives at IE University, and I would like to thank her for her dedication and commitment. Additionally, the IE University Center for Social Innovation, led by Concepción Galdón, has continued with this approach, enriching the curriculum of all our programs. Sustainability is embedded in our institution's culture.

The formidable institutional relations team that works alongside me has helped select the candidates whose stories I hope will inspire my readers. I would particularly like to express my appreciation for their assistance to Ana de la Cruz, Head of Institutional Relations, Felicia Appenteng, Chair of the IE Africa Center, and Geoffroy Gerard, Associate Director of the IE Foundation.

Similarly, the communication department at IE University has always been at my side in advising me in my knowledge-generation and dissemination activities, and I would especially like to mention Yolanda Regodón, Kerry Parke, Igor Galo, Pablo Sun Li, Isabel Macías and Verónica Urbiola.

Nor can I fail to mention my gratitude to Cynthia Fernández Lázaro, Director of IE Publishing, Irene Jayo Garitocelaya, my Personal Assistant, for their inestimable aid in bringing this book into the world, along with the support and suggestions of my editor at Palgrave Macmillan, Liz Barlow.

I also owe thanks to two of my academic colleagues in my early years as researcher of jurisprudence and moral philosophy, Jerónimo Betegón and Juan Ramón de Páramo.

I would like to express a few final words of profound gratitude to three people without whose permanent support I would not have been able to write this book: José Félix Valdivieso, my talented friend and chief of staff, who helped me from the first moment to conceptualize this work, while advising me on its focus and contents; Nick Lyne, my translator and English editor with whom I have worked closely on all my books for a number of years; and finally, Juan Ramón Zamorano, to whom I dedicate this book and with whom I have read and corrected all the chapters as they were written.

How to Read This Book

This book explores the contribution of a select group of female philosophers to the field of management. The objective is to provide an accessible introduction to their philosophical ideas and models and to illustrate their use in the day-to-day running of companies and interpersonal relations in the wider world of business.

I have chosen these philosophers for their relevance, rather than for any academic relationship, with the specific intention of covering a range of cultures, themes and outlooks. By the same token, my choice of women from business and non-commercial institutions was based on the same criteria of diversity.

Each chapter begins or ends with a profile of a woman from business or a major institution, chosen for her achievements or potential. The central part of each chapter is dedicated to a female philosopher and some of her ideas and how they can be applied to management. The chapters end with a number of takeaways, underpinning the applicability of the philosophy under review.

The chapters can be read independently, on the basis of the reader's interest, or sequentially.

Bearing in mind that this is a book about philosophy, my objective is to open my readers' minds to new concepts and basic questions, rather than providing answers. Nevertheless, each chapter ends with a series of takeaways to help apply the ideas to actual business situations.

My hope is that readers enjoy reading this book as much as I have enjoyed writing it.

Contents

1	Why Female Philosophers Matter to Management: Randi Zuckerberg	1
2	*Balance*: Patricia Churchland/Belinda Holdsworth	19
3	*Courage*: Ayn Rand/Jiang Qiong Er	33
4	*Virtue*: Philippa Foot/Angelica Kohlmann	47
5	*Love*: Iris Murdoch/María Benjumea	61
6	*Authenticity*: Elizabeth Anscombe/Catherine Moukheibir	75
7	*Humanity*: Martha Nussbaum/Olga Urbani	91
8	*Fortitude*: Hannah Arendt/Maria Tereza Leme Fleury	107
9	*Passion*: Simone Weil/Michelle Raymond	121
10	*Ethics*: Adela Cortina/Inés Temple	135

11 *Vision*: Simone de Beauvoir/Usha Prashar   151

12 *Resolve*: African Challenges/Ifeoma Idigbe   167

Index   173

The Cast

Some light brushstrokes of the protagonists of this book.

Philosophy

Gertrude Elisabeth Margaret (G.E.M.) Anscombe (1919, UK–2001, UK) was a prominent figure of Analytical Thomism and a translator and literary executor of Ludwig Wittgenstein's work. She was a professor at the University of Cambridge and was a strong supporter of Catholic morals.

Hannah Arendt (1906, Germany–1975, United States) fled her native country after the Nazis came to power for the United States, where she worked for the Jewish Cultural Reconstruction. Her book *The Origins of Totalitarianism* (1951) consolidated her reputation as a leading contemporary thinker. She taught at many US universities and wrote on different topics, including democracy, human rights, morals and politics.

Simone de Beauvoir (1908, France–1986, France) was a contemporary existentialist philosopher and a successful novelist. Her book *The Second Sex* is considered a seminal work on feminism and feminist philosophy. Her novel *The Mandarins* won the Goncourt Prize. She was also involved in different political and societal causes.

Adela Cortina (1947, Spain) is an emeritus professor of Ethics at the University of Valencia, and head of the Etnor Foundation, which focuses on business ethics. Her book *Aporophobia: The Rejection of the Poor* (2017) offers alternative reasons for the underlying causes of xenophobia and racism in Europe.

Patricia Churchland (1943, Canada) is a renowned auhtor on neurophilosophy and is UC President's Professor of Philosophy Emerita at the University of California, San Diego. Her latest book is *Conscience: The Origins of Moral Intuition* (2019).

Philippa Foot (1920, UK–2010, UK) is considered one of the contemporary founders of Virtue Ethics and was affiliated to the University of Oxford and the University of California, Los Angeles. She was the author of *Virtues and Vices and Other Essays in Moral Philosophy* (1978).

Iris Murdoch (1919, Ireland–1999, UK) received more recognition in life as a novelist than a philosopher. Her novel *The Sea, The Sea* won the Booker Prize. She was also conferred the Golden PEN Award for her services to literature. She taught at Oxford University and London's Royal College of Arts.

Martha Nussbaum (1943, United States) is Ernst Freund Distinguished Service Professor of Law and Ethics at the University of Chicago and has received multiple awards for her defense of the role of Humanities in higher education. Her latest book is *The Monarchy of Fear: A Philosopher Looks at Our Political Crisis* (2018).

Ayn Rand (1905, Russia–1982, United States) is associated with libertarianism and laissez-faire capitalism and founded a movement called Objectivism. Her two best-known novels are *The Fountainhead* (1943) and *Atlas Shrugged* (1957).

Simone Weil (1909, France–1943, UK) was considered in life more a mystic and a political activist than a philosopher. Her experiences with the republicans at the Spanish Civil War, working at a Renault factory and at a war hospital, where she died, provided with first-hand materials for her varied philosophical writings on work, labor and society.

Management

Maria Benjumea (Spain) is an entrepreneur, founder and CEO of Spain Start-Up and South Summit, a global innovation platform for entrepreneurs, investors and business stakeholders.

The Cast

Maria Tereza Fleury (Brazil) is the former Dean at the business schools of both the University of Sao Paulo and the EAESP Fundação Getulio Vargas. She researches and publishes on international business.

Belinda Holdsworth (UK) is Head of Global Operations Strategy at Roche and is involved in different initiatives related to the promotion of women and a range of social causes.

Ifeoma Idigbe (Nigeria) is a founder and executive vice-chairman of boys to Men foundation, as well as Chairman of the Board of WIMBIZ, Women in Management, Business & Public Service.

Angelica Kohlmann (Austria) is Chairman and CEO of her family holding Kohlmann & Co AG, Switzerland, focused on tech and biotech start-ups, and Chair of the Board of the Global Peter Drucker Forum.

Catherine Moukheibir (Lebanon) is currently Chairman and CEO of MedDay Pharmaceuticals (France) and non-executive director of four other businesses in the biotech and pharmaceutical sectors.

Usha Prashar (UK) is a crossbench member of the House of Lords and has held leading positions at different non-governmental organizations, including the Chair at the National Council for Voluntary Organizations and the British Council.

Jiang Qiong Er (China) is the founder and CEO of Shang Xia, a joint venture with French company Hermes, focused on premium products that combine Chinese tradition and quality.

Michelle Raymond (United States) is a musician, currently studying at Berklee School of Music. She was previously the leader of Morgan Stanley's Wealth Management pride network team.

Inés Temple (Peru) is CEO of LHH-DBM Peru and Chair of the Board of LHH Chile, one of the leading companies in outplacement and talent development in the region. She is also an investor.

Olga Urbani (Italy) is CEO of Urbani Tartufi, the world's leading truffle company. She has been awarded different prizes for her dedication to social causes.

Randi Zuckerberg (United States) is the founder of Zuckerberg Media (United States) and editor-in-chief of Dot Complicated. She was the first director of marketing at Facebook and is the author of several books.

1

Why Female Philosophers Matter to Management: Randi Zuckerberg

An Unforgivable Absence

We professors learn a lot from our students, sometimes as much or more than they do from us. Reverse learning is an inestimable and very agreeable facet of teaching, and, if we're lucky, it happens in each class that we teach.

Two years ago, I had one of those unforgettable experiences in my first session with the students of the Global MBA at IE Business School, a program that combines residential periods with synchronous and asynchronous sessions. I teach in this program because it's compatible with my busy agenda of meetings and frequent trips. The same applies to many of the students, young executives with an average of ten years of managerial experience, and who are located across continents and represent a unique diversity of origin, gender and visions of the world.

At the opening session of the program, after remarking on the diversity of students in the class while explaining the case studies we were going to use on the course, Corporate and Competitive Strategy, one student, white British and male, pointed out that all the CEOs of the companies to be analyzed were "male and western." I undertook the commitment on the spot to make the necessary changes in the program and did so that same night.

I recall that as an accreditor at European Foundation for Management Development (EFMD), one of the frequent criticisms of MBA program content is the preponderance of case studies of large US companies and the absence of case studies on SMEs and companies from other countries. When I designed my program, I had managed to include cases of European and

Latin American companies of different sizes, but none of the key players were women.

That night, a quick search for cases of General Management and Strategy with female CEOs provided some interesting results. For example, a recent study by Harvard Business Publishing (HBP) shows that only 11% of the cases of its directory, the most widely used in the world, have a female CEO or director and that most of them were related to organizational behavior typically dealing with the glass ceiling syndrome.[1] Under the category General Management or Strategy, I was able to find only a recent case that would fit the themes of my course, related to Ginni Rometty, CEO of IBM, and the launch of the Watson project.

There's no denying that there are few cases, teaching materials or academic research reflecting diversity in companies, whether gender or otherwise. To a large degree, this reflects the same lack of diversity in companies, where much remains to be done to achieve gender equity, for example, in areas related to selection, promotion, compensation and other forms of recognition.

However, the point the student was making was not just about the lack of diversity in case studies, but also the need for educators to be critical, to guide students toward a model of society and an ideal of the company we want to build. A lack of case studies is not a sufficient argument for not teaching the values and principles we want to instill in our students. To use an extreme example, a professor of political science who believes in democracy, but who unfortunately lives in a dictatorship, would not be satisfied with simply describing the authoritarian institutions around her, but would rather encourage her students to change them.

Similarly, the function of business schools is not just descriptive of explaining how companies work; they also have a critical and prescriptive role: that of developing models that should inspire entrepreneurs, models that can serve as a reference to make organizations not only be more effective, but also fairer.

Female CEOs are still a minority, but this is no excuse for business schools not to design programs with content that will inspire future generations of women and contribute to achieving a balance in the composition of management cadres. Such an approach can only be better for companies and for society.

Here are a few ideas business schools could think about implementing:

— Firstly, develop a greater awareness of the lack of gender diversity in companies, develop similar sensibilities to those of my student, with a strong instinct toward inclusion.

- Produce more case studies, especially in areas such as General Management and Strategy, with women taking the leading role. At IE University, we have started a project to create a catalog that includes cases in all business areas where decision makers are women.
- Improve gender diversity in the faculty. It is no surprise that the percentage of female professors in this field is low. Fortunately, IE Business School has one of the highest percentages of female teachers in the world: 40%.[2] We will continue improving this figure as part of a continuous process of improvement.
- Improve the subjects, methodologies and programs in business schools, promoting examples of women who serve as inspiration to young students.
- Facilitate initiatives that promote inclusion and opportunities for women to succeed in academic programs, with specific awards and recognitions. This could be supplemented with coaching or mentoring programs, where mentors can be women or men, such as the "He For She" initiative, committed to equitable business models.

I am hopeful: Over the years, I have seen growing numbers of students committed to transforming reality and achieving fairer social conditions. We will continue to learn from them in class, because teaching is a mutually enriching experience.

One of the goals of this book is to share the inspiring stories of women from the world of business and institutions and that they will serve as a reference for upcoming managers, both men and women. I have selected people I know and admire, who have shared their ideas and experiences with me first hand. The women I have chosen are from every continent and reflect a wide range of cultures and world views. I hope my readers can learn as much from these stories as I have.

Why Female Philosophers Have a Contribution to Make to Management

Management is philosophy in action. Underpinning any business strategy or key decision taken in a company is a conception of the world, a vision of how society should be, how we can improve life for everyone and how we should behave toward each other.

If the important decisions in companies and the behavior of their leaders presuppose a philosophy, a value system, then it is surely important to know, explore and articulate the values of the company or what you believe when you make a decision. An important part of leading a business consists in articulating the vision and values that inform its activity.

This is why it is so relevant to cultivate philosophy, to know the theories that have influenced the thinking, that have sought to provide a vision, a sense of human life and relationships in society. Over the course of history, philosophers have addressed a range of questions that are key in terms of both a personal perspective and business initiatives.

For example, moral philosophy tries to provide an answer to the question as to how to behave. Its approaches can provide solutions in the business decision-making process, which is fraught with moral dilemmas that managers and directors must navigate.

Epistemology can help us explain how we know what we know, as well as to understand the limits of knowledge. As has been pointed out on more than one occasion, we now live in a world with virtually limitless access to knowledge, and yet we are more uncertain than ever before.

Other disciplines related to applied philosophy, such as political philosophy or jurisprudence, aim to provide the means to build fairer social institutions or how to make us freer and more equal, thus improving the lives of people, but they may be also of use while designing fairer and sustainable business organizations.

Human evolution and the development of modern society have seen the appearance of new branches of philosophy that try to offer a rational explanation of the phenomena around us. For example, in recent years, neurophilosophy connects knowledge of the human brain provided by science with models explaining how our minds function or should function. Similarly, feminist philosophy's goal is to round out conventional philosophy with women's particular viewpoint, so long ignored throughout the history of thought, as well as introducing questions that are more relevant to women.

Philosophy aspires to transcend, and the aim of most philosophers has been to improve the world around them, to make the world a better place. That said, there's long been something lacking in philosophy, an unforgivable absence in today's world. Traditionally, philosophy has been one of the branches of the Humanities dominated by men.

Certain passages of some of the classic works of philosophy are, by today's standards, unacceptable in the way they refer to women. Socrates is reputed to have said that listening to his wife, Xanthippe, talk was akin to "tolerating the cackling of geese."[3] Perhaps the most revealing episode in the life of Socrates is mentioned in Plato's *Euthyphro*, when shortly before he was due to drink hemlock, Socrates dismissed Xanthippe, preferring to spend his last hours talking with his disciples.[4]

Immanuel Kant, arguably the leading philosopher of the Enlightenment, suggested that men and women had different strengths, "the understanding of the man and the taste of the wife."[5] In the nineteenth century, Schopenhauer wrote that women "remain big children, their whole lives long: a kind of intermediate stage between the child and the man, who is the actual human being, 'man'."[6]

We might usefully ask to what extent the great philosophers are responsible for the cultural discrimination suffered by women over the centuries, along with the attribution of female roles prevalent until just a few decades ago. As the philosopher Virginia Valiant notes: "Western philosophy was formed around an overlapping series of conceptual oppositions—reason/emotion, mind/body, culture/nature—coding a hierarchical understanding of the relationship of masculine and feminine that can be discerned throughout the 2,500-year history of the subject."[7]

This masculinization of philosophical debate, in terms of topics, conceptual frameworks and even language, has arguably dissuaded many women from entering the field. At the same time, it has spurred the creation of a new branch, feminist philosophy, which as mentioned earlier, is trying to make up for centuries of male domination.

Historically, there have been any number of relevant female philosophers, whose contribution is now attracting growing attention. The cases from Hypatia of Alexandria in the fifth century to Mary Wollstonecraft and Madame de Staël in the eighteenth century, along with many of the brilliant thinkers covered by this book, are evidence that women had to make much more effort to succeed in a field dominated by men. They might be seen as outliers, their work largely ignored by their male colleagues.[8]

Unfortunately, the gender imbalance in philosophy continues. Writing a decade ago, and citing a wide range of sources, Fiona Jenkins and Katrina Hutchison noted that just 21% of academic philosophers in the United States were women. At the same time, the number of women in prestigious institutions is disproportionately low, as is the ratio of articles by women in academic journals, other than those dedicated to feminism. The data isn't much more encouraging in Canada, where only 21% of full-time academics are women, or in Australia, where the figure for women in continuing positions in philosophy was 29%.[9]

Jenkins and Hutchinson sum up their findings thus: "Among the factors limiting change discussed in this volume are the influence of unconscious biases and the impact this has on women who internalize them (Jennifer Saul), the cumulative effect of micro-inequities (Samantha Brennan), the tendency to identify women's differences from men with deviance from an uncritically adopted norm (Helen Beebee), undergraduate teaching curricular (Marilyn Friedman) and methods (Katrina Hutchison), as well as systemic failures to recognize women as partners to discussion, leading to their effective 'silencing' within the discipline (Justine McGill)."[10]

As things stand, even with steady improvements, it would take many years to overcome these imbalances, as we have seen in other areas, such as the presence of women on boards or in senior management positions, as well as at university tenured positions, particularly since the academic world is known for its reluctance to change. Only through affirmative action initiatives, to improve gender diversity in academia, will we see any progress within a reasonable time frame.

This book aims to make a contribution to greater inclusion in the academic philosophy, as well as in business. I believe that the women selected here in the fields of philosophy and business serve as an inspiration for the men and women working for a more integrated, fair and supportive future.

Why Should Managers Philosophize?

Management is an action-oriented profession. One of the chief characteristics of a good manager is being able to take decisions quickly, manage meetings efficiently and generally drive improved productivity. Time is one of the scarcest and most valuable resources in the world of management and must thus be administered efficiently. Among the duties of a good chairman of the board is bringing the meetings she presides over to an end in good time and having covered all the topics on the agenda.

Equally, one of the competitive advantages that innovative companies try to develop is "time to market," the speed with which new services or products are made available to customers. Most business leaders would agree that his speed and ability to maximize use of time to the point when competitors copy products or services are the best way to protect an innovation. Agility and speed define the innovative director and successful companies.

But there is little time for reflection in a business world where opinions must be formed and decisions are taken on the hoof, and it seems counterintuitive to cultivate an interest in philosophy, an activity that requires stopping the clock and taking time to think things through. Philosophy addresses the basic questions of our existence, our identity, our role in the world and the models for living that might inspire our actions. It also prompts us to explore the fundamental values we share with the society we live in, such as ideals of liberty, justice and equality, liberal democracy, the law and the free market.

In our hyperconnected and technologized world, directors face a significant challenge finding the time for reflection, for the peaceful and considered introspection required for thinking about the really important issues, for making plans for the future, establishing objectives and deciding how we want to be and how our behavior can conform to that ideal. Some people use long plane journeys to find these moments of calm during which we can think about these important questions. Equally, we can take advantage of a weekend in the country to distance ourselves from the pressures of work and everyday life. There is also the option of joining a retreat led by a professional coach able to guide us through these questions; developing mindfulness techniques is another option.

Whichever approach we take, I believe that if we are to carry out our professional duties *and* function better at the emotional level, we need to find the balance between management's orientation toward action and thinking about our ideals, values and principles, which not only give meaning to life, but to our work, which is part of it. Reflection and action are not separate parts of our lives, but rather two sides of the same coin. As Iris Murdoch, one of the philosophers whose work is explored in this book, points out in *The Sovereignty of Good*: "The task of attention goes on all the time and at apparently empty and everyday moments we are 'looking', making those little efforts of imagination."[11] Almost unconsciously, we are permanently forming and recalibrating our system of personal values.

I believe that the presence of philosophy, of our values and principles, in every aspect of human life is unavoidable, including when we practice management. It is essential, therefore, that we understand that business decisions are not just based on neutral theories or impartial models, they also reflect a world view of how companies should operate; in short, they follow a certain philosophy of management. In fact, every management theory and every business model derive from assumptions about the function of companies and the role of managers, as well as from a broad picture about the meaning of business.

Even denying any connection between management and principles or values is a philosophical statement in itself, which may be associated with nihilism, cynicism or relativism, philosophical options that many thinkers disregard as self-refuting.[12]

Over recent years, business educators and executives have increasingly recognized the importance of building management theories and models on the basis of values and principles. The increasing awareness among all business stakeholders of the need to connect management and philosophy has encouraged business schools to introduce Humanities courses. At the same time, the literature on management and philosophy has experienced successful growth and been well received.

Ayn Rand, another of the philosophers analyzed in this book, illustrated this in her 1974 *Philosophy: who needs it?* speech at West Point "Without abstract ideas, you would not be able to deal with concrete, particular, real-life problems. You would be in the position of a newborn infant, to whom every object is a unique, unprecedented phenomenon. The difference between his mental state and yours lies in the number of conceptual integrations your mind has performed. You have no choice about the necessity to integrate your observations, your experiences, your knowledge into abstract ideas, i.e., into principles."[13]

Rand argues that what binds principles and values is philosophy:

> A philosophic system is an integrated view of existence. As a human being, you have no choice about the fact that you need a philosophy. Your only choice is whether you define your philosophy by a conscious, rational, disciplined process of thought and scrupulously logical deliberation — or let your subconscious accumulate a junk heap of unwarranted conclusions.[14] (14)

Therefore, if our behavior and our decisions at work and in our personal lives always respond to certain values and principles, might it not be a good idea to identify and analyze them, to make them more explicit, as well as to better understand if we are acting consistently or contradictorily?

Insights from a Committed Entrepreneur and Mom: Randi Zuckerberg[15]

I held this interview with Randi Zuckerberg, founder of Zuckerberg Media (United States) and editor-in-chief of Dot Complicated, in the summer of 2019. Randi was also the first director of marketing development at Facebook, the company founded by her brother Mark. I decided to use the interview in its entirety, since it provides many valuable insights for the upcoming generation of female entrepreneurs and managers.

> *Santiago Iniguez (SI)*: In some interviews, you have referred to your mother as a role model. Some women who opt for a fast track career sometimes feel guilty for not devoting enough time to their children. How important is it for mothers to provide an inspirational model as successful professionals to their daughters? What advice would you give to young mothers who have to combine demanding jobs with bringing up children?

1 Why Female Philosophers Matter to Management: Randi Zuckerberg

Randi Zuckerberg (RZ): My mother wasn't always my number one role model. Growing up I wanted to sing under the big, bright lights of Broadway so I had dreams of becoming the next Carol Channing, Patti LuPone or Mary Martin…. and my mother was anything but a piano bar diva. Sure, she was a psychologist fulfilling dreams of her own, but our two career choices couldn't have been any more different. While I admired her for building such a successful self-practice, I didn't see how following in my mother's footsteps (something she was constantly pushing for) could've got me closer to the Great White Way. I thought our goals had nothing in common. But all that changed when I applied to Harvard.

At Harvard I couldn't major in musical theater without a whole slough of prerequisites I didn't have—and wouldn't have—until my sophomore or junior year *maybe*. I needed a major to get into school and there was nothing that really interested me because I had my eyes on the prize of Broadway.

My mother encouraged me to follow her own path and major in psychology because, as she put it, psychology applies to EVERYTHING—from the personal to the professional too, yes, even the inner workings of the theater. I listened to my mom's advice and majored in psychology. And now, if it weren't for her guidance, I wouldn't be where I am today. So I do believe that sometimes the old adage of 'moms really do know best' *can* be true, but we also have to remember that not all moms are working throughout their child's development.

Going back to my own mom, she gave up that same successful practice to raise us four kids. When we were old enough, she went back to work, but for years she gave up something she deeply loved for something she loved even more: Us. So while it's important for mothers to be inspirational role models to their daughters, it's important to remember not all moms are successful professionals, or professionals at all. Everyone's path is different and moms come in all packages—both working and stay-at-home. However a mother chooses to take care of her kids doesn't make their advice any less or more valid.

Which is why the one piece of advice I'd give to busy, working moms, and stay at home moms alike, is to take care of your family the best way YOU can, not how anyone else does it. I have to travel over 100+ days a year for work, which means being away from my three kids. It's something I not only have to do to take care of my family, but I also enjoy doing too. Another mom might never want to travel without her family. It doesn't invalidate either of our choices. It's how we both do the best we can to be good mothers while taking care of our own needs.

Do what's right for you and your family. There's no one size fits all manual for being a mom.

> *SI*: You were the first member of your family to attend an Ivy League college, and the only one to graduate from Harvard. What advice would you give to young women who aspire to join elite universities and colleges from less-affluent families?
>
> *RZ*: I didn't get into Harvard because my parents had any connection or influence with the school. I only had lofty aspirations and wasn't willing to take 'no' for an answer. Plus, everyone from my high school counselor to yes, even my mom, didn't think I'd ever make it into Harvard U. My grades weren't up to snuff, I wasn't a straight A student or a starter on a division-winning sports team. I was a theater nerd who played tournament bridge, sang in theater camps, caddied at the bridge club and volunteered with the elderly. Thankfully all my outside interests were what got me into Harvard because the admissions officer said they needed more "interesting" people like myself to balance out the high-performing achievers who were more focused on books. It was my *lopsidedness* that got me in an elite school, not a 4.0+ average.

I was definitely lucky to have parents who had the money to afford to send us kids to any college—much less elite ones. I know that financial issues are what hold many prospective students back from attending the college of their dreams, so my advice would be to make sure you that have a lot of outside interests, as I did, that can help, not only get you in your dream school, but also help get you financial aid in the form of scholarships.

In the years leading up to your college admission, scour the internet for scholarship opportunities to apply for. There's money available EVERYWHERE you just have to look. I have a friend who got her Masters and helped pay for her schooling with small $100–$1000 scholarships for criteria that she fit the bill for. Also, ask your place of worship, your job, your high school—whoever will listen—to help you afford books or tuition. It's all about having the mindset of not giving up or letting anyone tell you what you can or can't do.

> *SI*: Among your passions are music and singing, and you were an active member of an a cappella choir at Harvard. How important is music and the Humanities in developing our personality and complementing formal education?
>
> *RZ*: We are who we are through the way we express ourselves, this means the music we love and the art we create are crucial to personal growth. But

enjoying the humanities is more than going to the theater or a museum. Since the beginning of time politics, the state of world affairs, personal struggles and emotions — everything — has been expressed through art.

Art is taught to children at the youngest of ages to not only expand their creativity and imagination, but also help them progress with their own mental development. 2001's No Child Left Behind Act listed art as a core academic subject while data from the Turnaround Arts program showed that schools with mandatory art classes experienced a 22.5% increase in math scores, a 12.6% improvement in reading scores, and an overall increase in standardized testing to boot!

Art helps therapeutically, too. Trauma, hypertension, PTSD can all be minimized through creating and enjoying art. Cutting arts and music funding in schools is detrimental to both children and society at large. Art is subjective yet it's still a great connector. Music brings people closer to other cultures. Our personalities depend on art. That's why STEM programs are created as STEAM programs with that ever-important A for the arts.

> *SI*: Some careers seem more challenging for women. STEM degree studies have a long way in achieving gender balance. What recommendations would you make to educators to promote diversity and inclusion, particularly in STEM subjects?
>
> *RZ*: A wonderful way to promote diversity and inclusion in every industry, boardroom, classroom, or sector is by HIRING MORE WOMEN! A 2014 MIT study on workplace diversity shows that business revenue can increase by as much as 41% when offices are split evenly along gender lines. Which means if ALL women get a chance to work to their full potential and have an equal role to men, they can add an extra $29 TRILLION to the global GDP by 2025!

Another way to promote inclusion and diversity is by holding blind interviews, which means applicants take their names off their resume to eradicate any sort of gender or racial bias that may have existed in the hiring process. This way a person is hired based solely on their experience.

It's important for educators to teach the importance of inclusion and diversity by enacting practices like these. From blind applications to hiring and promoting more women in leadership roles, students and sponsors alike will benefit. The data proves it!

> *SI*: In the 1970s and 1980s some Scandinavian countries implemented drastic affirmative action and reverse discrimination policies, including quotas,

that have resulted in what is probably the fairest and most inclusive societies anywhere. Most governments have been headed or dominated by women there as well. Do you support quotas or positive affirmation policies to achieve fairer gender balance, particularly in senior positions?

RZ: Absolutely 100% yes! I am totally behind lawmakers getting more women into leadership roles. With a measly 22% of women making up all the CEOs in the Fortune 500, former Governor Jerry Brown signed a legislation making California the first state to require publically traded companies to have at least one female on their board of directors. Companies that don't comply with the law will be fined $100,000 and further violations will draw a $300,000 fine. Sounds tough but how many qualified women have already been passed over to keep the old boys' network going? Jerry Brown is definitely onto something BIG!

Then there are companies who are taking matters into their own hands without needing any legislation. Like Amazon, who adopted the NFL's Rooney Rule, a policy put in place to put at least one minority candidate up for consideration in an open leadership role. Amazon adopted the Rooney Rule into its boardroom last year and now there are three women on the board.

Data proves inclusion and diversity helps business benefit and I support anything, whether it's a law, a rule or an initiative, that gives women a seat at the table.

SI: You have written two books for children, the protagonists of which are girls. How can we instill in young children an open mindset toward diversity and inclusion?

RZ: It all starts with education. Just as art helps develop the personality and imagination, learning to embrace diversity is just as crucial. Educators should teach diverse family traditions in the classroom. Kids are curious about those who don't follow the same holidays as they do. When classrooms celebrate other cultures, children learn that differences are every bit as much of a strength as similarities are.

Kids should also be able to talk about the things that make them unique, which is why show and tell time is not only a good exercise on public speaking, but it's good for kids' self-esteem to discuss what makes them interesting and different. Show and tell is also a wonderful way to allow other kids to ask questions when some parents and adults would shut them down for being rude. Kids are inquisitive. Having open conversations about differences help normalize differences and makes children more accepting and respectful.

Personally, when I write children's books, it's important that I, as the author, set a good example myself. I make my characters, like Dot and Missy President, diverse and empathetic to create good role models for kids to see themselves in. I believe that the earlier we start children down the path of acceptance and enthusiasm for diversity, the sooner we can create a world where everyone is heard and valued.

> *SI*: You are an entrepreneur and have founded two media companies. You have also been involved in other leading businesses, including Facebook, where you made key contributions to its success. How can we foster an entrepreneurial spirit among young women?
>
> *RZ*: No one gets to the top alone so it's important for young women to have good mentors. But getting access to those good mentors is not quite as easy as it sounds. Sure, women can email a female leader they admire and ask to pick her brain for a bit, but studies show that it's continuous access to good mentors that leads to better salaries, better jobs, and overall happiness for women in business.

So how do young women find and retain good mentors? One way is through their schools and colleges. By asking a teacher they admire or their school counselor to help match them to a mentor, young ladies can find reliable and trustworthy mentors that are already validated. Also joining women's groups such as Young Entrepreneurs Across America, Ladies Who Launch, or even Facebook's 80,000-plus membered Like-Minded Bitches Drinking Wine can help provide access to peer-based mentors… and wine!

Another way is by joining more professional networks, which is one of the many reasons I launched my growth accelerator, Zuckerberg Institute. At Zuckerberg Institute we connect founders and business leaders with, not only myself, but also to some of the women who help mentor ME, like author and venture capitalist, Fran Hauser and Sally Kohn. These women have helped my own portfolio grow so I think it's important to pass their invaluable expertise and advice onto others looking to further their career.

> *SI*: Many business schools still lack a fair proportion of women in their programs, particularly MBAs and Executive MBAs. What recommendations would you make to business educators to improve diversity and inclusion in business schools?
>
> *RZ*: We've heard of CEOs, CMOs and CFOs, but most businesses and business schools are lacking a CDO — a Chief Diversity Officer. Business schools that have adopted the CDO position, like the Terry College of

Business at the University of Georgia and the Jesse H. Jones Graduate School of Business at Rice University, have seen an uptick in a more diverse student population and more high-value employers seeking out their students for work. Which means the chances of getting hired upon graduation are that much higher just for going to school!

There's also the Graduate Management Admission Council that has a Diversity Advisory Group that business schools can utilize to help identify the best practices necessary for recruiting and retaining a diverse student body.

Like diversity and inclusion advocate, Juliane Iannarelli, says, business schools that implement diversity strategies will positively influence not only transactional outcomes like increasing the number of underrepresented students, but will also embed inclusion into all matters of business education, furthering meaningful and productive careers for everyone. It's what trickle down economics should be!

> *SI*: Interestingly, only 11% of case studies published by Harvard Business Publishing have female protagonists, and mostly related to the "glass ceiling" syndrome, but very few with female CEOs as the main characters. Do we need more inspiring case studies on women like yourself?
>
> *RZ*: I had the pleasure of hosting the Founder and Director of the Annenberg Inclusion Initiative, Dr. Stacy L. Smith, on my weekly SiriusXM business show, *Dot Complicated with Randi Zuckerberg*. Dr. Smith is a known for her work in social change, closing the gender gap and of course her detailed studies on inclusion in different areas of media.

Dr. Smith was also the creator of the Inclusion Rider, which is now used in many blockbuster films to ensure women are paid their worth which is equal or more to that of their male counterparts. Her work has been crucial in changing the inequality landscape in Hollywood, so imagine what more case studies highlighting the inequality women face in business could do!

I believe that we learn from our mistakes—and also that history repeats itself. To forever close the gender gap in business we need to hear more about the businesses that got it right, how it benefited their profits and how their bottom line of inclusion and diversity helped change the general landscape of how their business scaled to unimagined heights.

Instead of focusing on what's wrong with gender equality we're taking away from what's right, like the Boston Consulting Group study which found that out of 1700 companies across 8 different countries, increasing diversity resulted in 19% higher profits due to innovation. Or the fact that

30% of small and growing businesses are run by women. Or the fact that women control over $20 trillion of global spending and make 80% of the buying decisions. We need more women like Dr. Stacy to create more case studies, to provide more data, and to offer solutions to show that gender inclusion is, indeed, great for business.

> *SI*: In your experience, what are the most important skills for a successful female CEO?

I think the most important skill for all CEOs is to be a good listener. You can't delegate or lead if you can't hear the needs of your employers and customers. Which goes hand in hand with being able to appreciate critical feedback. Anyone can praise your company and tell you how great you are, but there's a time and a place for positive feedback.

A good CEO, man or woman, must be able to understand the criticism they receive and then, in turn, know what to do with it. Making changes, pivoting, restructuring are all part of the CEO's duty. If you are unwilling to budge on areas that need attention, eventually other pieces of your business puzzle are going to get lost as well.

I believe having a fun, positive outlook directly feeds company morale. It can't be all profit-making all the time. Employees need to feel appreciated, heard, and inspired. A good CEO can do all of these things simply by wearing their enthusiasm on their sleeve.

Once you layer on more responsibility, profit margins, employee trust, and everything else on top of an already stressful position, it's easy for CEOs to forget we've all worked for someone else ourselves once before. If we allow our employees to make mistakes, ask questions, and simply breathe, we'll get better performances from our team.

But the number one skill that female CEOs need to cultivate is the art of saying NO—something that women across the board often struggle with. Women have been taught the outdated notion that asking for and saying what we want is somehow bitchy, yet nothing could be further from the truth. So a trick I've learned when I'm feeling shaky about a tough decision is to ask myself, "What would my male colleagues do?" Chances are he'd do exactly what I was ready to do in the first place.

> *SI*: You mention Steve Forbes in one of your books, and his support while you were a panelist on Forbes on Fox. You also refer to an unfortunate episode with your female boss at Ogilvy How relevant is mentorship in facilitating women's access to top management?

RZ: One of my favorite business books of the year is Fran Hauser's *Myth of the Nice Girl*. In her book Fran breaks down the stereotype that nice women have to struggle to get ahead and shatters the perception that there's only room for one woman at the table at the time. It's bad business beliefs like these that hold women back. Which is why it's so important that women at the top help women on their way up.

As I mentioned previously, this is best done through reliable, trustworthy mentorship. Finding peers and mentors who can help you get ahead with a business mindset is crucial to your attitude and outlook in the workplace. Becoming a boss is more than a job title. We get where we are by learning how to react, act, and be more authentic. And the way we learn those skills are by experience and good leadership. It's important for women at the top to lead by example, and kindness and paying it forward are two of the most important skills successful leaders have.

SI: Would you like to share any personal experience or anecdote that may be helpful for other women in management?

RZ: As I often say in my business keynotes around the world, with a smartphone in our pocket, each and every one of us is now our own media company. So I think it's important to always remember who you are IS your brand. And the best way to be the most effective leader is to unapologetically wear your personal brand on your sleeve and lead that way.

For example, I love musical theater, Instagram, selfies and all things glitter so I embrace my personal brand of whimsy, imagination and awkwardness. Therefore all of the companies I create embrace those same aspects of myself. From my family-friendly, STEM-themed, interactive pop-up restaurant, Sue's Tech Kitchen, to my Broadway venture capital firm, Broadway Beta Ventures, I lead by living authentically at all times.

There's no shame in being wholly you at the workplace. Your employees will appreciate you all the more for it and you'll be a better, happier leader in the process!

Notes

1. L. Symons, Only 11% of Top Business School Studies Have a Female Protagonist, *Harvard Business Review*, March 9, 2016.

    The author suggests that "Clearing houses should publicize and reward cases with diverse characters. If you can measure it, you can start to change it. Data in this area is crucial. Case clearing houses, such as the Case Centre or Harvard, can assist by actively bringing the topic into the open. They could start by tracking the gender — and ethnicity — of the protagonist and making this information visible on their websites."

An interesting contribution providing data on women in business and analysis: C. Criado Pérez, "Invisible Women: Data Bias in a World Designed for Men" (New York, NY: Abrams Press, 2019).

2. Updated figures on the percentage of female faculty members, students and board members at business schools are provided on annual basis by *The Financial Times* rankings. http://rankings.ft.com/businessschoolrankings/global-mba-ranking-2019.

3. K. Hutchinson and F. Jenkins (eds.), *Women In Philosophy: What Needs to Change?* (Oxford: Oxford University Press, 1993); p. 2.

A very interesting philosophy blog worth following, edited by Maria Popova, is "Brain Pickings," where the Bulgarian writer and philosopher contributes on different thinkers and ideas. https://www.brainpickings.org.

4. Plato, *Phaedo* (Oxford: Oxford University Press, 1995); 57a–60b writes that Crito, a disciple of Socrates, took Xanthippe out of his room just hours before taking the hemlock, since she had started to cry and beat her chest when his disciples entered.

5. I. Kant, *Observations on the Feeling of the Beautiful and Sublime and Other Writings*, Frierson and Guyer (eds. and trans.) (Cambridge, UK: Cambridge University Press, 2011); p. 249.

6. A. Schopenhauer, *Essays and Aphorisms*, Hollingdale (trans.). (London and New York: Penguin, 1970); p. 81.

7. K. Hutchinson and F. Jenkins (eds.), op.cit., p. 2.

8. Two books are worth mentioning here: the classical anthology of M. Warnock (ed.), *Women Philosophers* (London: Orion Publishing Group-Everyman, 1996), which includes some of the thinkers reviewed in this book, and the monumental work in four books, from which I used: M.E. Waithe, *A History of Women Philosophers*, Vol. 4/1900-Today (Dordrecht, NL: Kluwer Academic Publishers, 1994).

9. K. Hutchinson and F. Jenkins (eds.), op.cit., p. 7. Interestingly, in the business world, the diagnosis on the lack of women in senior positions depends on whether you ask women or men. Sarah Green Carmichael describes this phenomenon, identified in a McKinsey report: *Where Women See Bias, Men See a 'Pipeline Problem'. McKinsey's enormous dataset shows diverging opinions on what stalls young women's careers.* Bloomberg, October 16, 2019. https://www.bloomberg.com/opinion/articles/2019-10-16/gender-bias-in-the-workplace-or-a-pipeline-problem.

On the obstacles women face on the early stages of their careers, see also: Vanessa Fuhrmans, Where Women Fall Behind at Work: The First Steps Into Management. Well before the glass ceiling, women run into

obstacles to advancement. Evening the odds in their careers would have a huge impact. *Wall Street Journal*, October 15, 2019. https://www.wsj.com/articles/where-women-fall-behind-at-work-the-first-step-into-management-11571112361.
10. Ibid.
11. I. Murdoch, *The Sovereignty of the Good* (London: Routledge & Kegan Paul, 1979); p. 35.
12. Vid., for example, H. Zellner, Is Relativism Self-Defeating? 20 *Journal of Philosophical Research* (1995), 287–295.
13. A. Rand, "Philosophy: Who Needs It?" (New York, NY: Penguin; Signet, 1984); p. 5.
14. Ibid.
15. This interview between Randi Zuckerberg and the author follows a written exchange and took place in September 2019.

2

Balance: Patricia Churchland/Belinda Holdsworth

What Distinguishes Humans from Robots?[1]

If you've seen the original, Oscar-winning *Blade Runner*, you'll know it's set in a future where humans live alongside replicants, androids that are only distinguishable from us by complex personality tests. The hero is a blade runner, who hunts replicants that have gone rogue, and of course falls in love with one, after all, he's a replicant too. The idea was explored more recently in the television series *Westworld* and is one that has fascinated us down through the ages: In the Iliad, Hephaestus creates two golden maidens to keep him company, while Ovid, in Metamorphosis, tells the story of Pygmalion, who falls in love with a statue he has made and brings her to life.

However, we should know by now that reality will always outdo fiction, which is why we ought to give some thought that at some point in the future, the development of artificial intelligence and machine learning will allow us to create robots that will be so perfect, physically and emotionally, that we could fall in love with them. Perhaps this would be the real Turing Test[2]: whether a machine could seduce a human into falling in love with it.

Similarly, in a future we may not live to see, given the progress of research in the pharma industry, biology, medicine and neuroscience, we may have access to drugs that segregate the hormones linked to our emotions, our sociability and our social instincts. These drugs would help us perform better, to be more or less aggressive, more friendly and perhaps better leaders.

That said, maybe we should also accept that it's not just their virtues, physical and intellectual, that attracts us to our fellow humans, but their defects, even if we often curse them. We're not ready for perfection, for endless virtue and would soon be bored; flawlessness is fine for contemplation, but not for interaction. The same applies to somebody who has taken drugs: They seem distant, enhanced and distorted.

I discussed these issues with Belinda Holdsworth, Head of Global Operations Strategy at Roche. Holdsworth has a degree in Biochemical Engineering from University College London and an Executive MBA from IE Business School. She has lived in Europe, Asia and the United States, having worked for Jacobs Engineering and Novartis before joining the Swiss multinational healthcare company, where she has also developed a number of social innovation projects.

On the question of transforming human potential, Holdsworth notes: "I guess we are already there, in the way that we do have drugs that influence our moods and our mental health.

> What would be the next step? To influence our performance, or our ability to work, does that make us less or more human? What is it that makes us human? Is it maybe the connection to our emotions, so that if we override that, we lose our individuality and just become robots? I would need to think about what the driver would be for that. Obviously, we already have mood-influencing drugs, like antidepressants, which address mental health issues, and if we're going beyond that and saying we want to remove the emotional variant in us, there are consequences. There's certainly a sense we can do that, and as leaders our responsibility and understanding of how our emotions impact our decisions and our perceptions of the world, how we react to others' behavior, and maybe that is something these drugs would influence as well. What makes us human beings and living creatures and what makes us robots that function, and why we would want to change that?

> I think our ability to be successful and creative in a working environment is based more on our social and psychological capabilities and competences rather than our work, which is technical: my early career was based on my understanding of engineering which is now irrelevant. It is about my ability to understand people, connect with people and provide for people that matters now. It goes back to us being humans as opposed to robots that don't do emotion. I think it is really important that as humans we understand ourselves and our emotions and everything we carry and the fact that our experience of life is mainly based on our experiences, our perception of life, of the experience we have had, the journey we have made and of what we have here. How we react to things is entirely based on that."

The pharmaceutical sector is no exception regarding the widespread lack of women in positions of authority, whereas in healthcare overall, women overwhelmingly occupy what we might call frontline posts in providing services and interaction with the client. I was interested in Holdsworth's experiences and whether she might provide inspiration to other female executives in her position. "This is an interesting question, because in my personal life, I participate in a particularly male-dominated sport, endurance sports, so I have spent much of my life in a very male-dominated world, and the same applies to my career over the last two decades.

> At this point, it actually feels very natural to me and if I were in an environment where the majority were women, I might feel it was unusual, out of the ordinary. But I think it's important to be yourself and to be comfortable with who you are, that's what makes you unique. Early in my career, I don't think people knew how to take me. I even worked on construction sites, I was this lonely woman in a very masculine culture and men had no clue what to do with me, how to interact with me, how to communicate with me, and I knew that I had to prove myself and my competence, my capabilities. They are not just going to accept me as someone who knows what they are talking about, because I'm not what they're expecting to see, but I think as I've got older, I get that less and less, I've learnt to build resilience.
>
> There is always a sense of being questioned, that I'm not part of the tribe, and that naturally build the feeling that I've earned my place at the table. I have a lot to offer and so, I guess that has helped me, but it's been a journey and I think it is a challenge that women face in male-dominated environments and probably vice versa. If you are the outlier in the situation, you have to prove yourself. You have to earn your place in the tribe. At this point, I'm so used to it, I don't even notice it anymore. It's clear I'm going to be the only woman here. There's still definitely a special connection with other women at that level, though. It's nice when you see another woman there. You do kind of connect, you know, 'I get you, I know how hard you have worked to get here'."

As part of her pro bono work, Holdsworth is involved in a number of initiatives, both inside and outside Roche, and is particularly interested in diversity and inclusion issues. For example, she leads a scheme within Roche to support women's development, which means identifying women with high potential and then using external coaches to form coaching circles within the company. "Our initial goal was four circles and then the women that took part would become mentors themselves and would use what they learnt during that process to build the network and build the circle.

We had women who were coached in challenging each other and in creating a strong network, supporting each other, and ensuring that they pushed each other to the next step. I am happy that at this stage the initiative has definitely been a success. In the first round, some women who joined said they wanted to move to a different part of the organization, which they achieved that. It was quite powerful when you have these networks and a trusted circle of people that you can go to and be open about things. Yes, I want to take this step and I'm not scared to admit it here, and a group of women that will help you achieve it. This is really helpful in the isolated environment women work in."

Holdsworth's commitment to helping women in her company develops their potential earned her an IE University Alumni Association's 2019 EPIC Awards nomination.

In this chapter, we will continue our conversation on how human potential can be further developed through science and technology and how philosophy can provide some answers in facing these questions.

The North Pole of Philosophy

The brain is the North Pole of scientists and philosophers: still largely unexplored, contested across a range of disciplines and a source of rich resources. We might have a better understanding of how we think, decide and behave if we knew more about the composition and functioning of our brain, but much of it is uncharted territory.

In recent years, a growing range of disciplines have begun exploring how our brains work, and one of the newest and most interesting is neurophilosophy, which posits that mental states, such as our thoughts, memories and feelings, have a physicochemical origin within the brain. For example, the happiness we experience when we see a loved one after an absence happens because our brain secretes certain hormones, specifically oxytocin and vasopressin, which make us more sociable, empathic and cheerful. These processes typically involve different areas of the brain: Neurons receive visual information through electrical impulses from the optic nerve; the ability to recall information is provided by memory, along with many other neuronal interactions or synapses, all of which take place within milliseconds.

Among the philosophers who have begun to look for answers about our behavior within neuroscience is Patricia Churchland. Currently, professor emeritus at the University of California, San Diego, where she has taught since 1984, Churchland previously studied at the University of British

Columbia in her native Canada, then at Pittsburgh and notably at Oxford. Her involvement in Oxford's philosophical community left its mark, as I can attest from personal experience, and Churchland would meet some of the thinkers included in this book, along with other eminent contemporary philosophers.

Her interest in neuroscience was awakened when teaching at the University of Manitoba in the 1970s, where she worked with the physiology department. Later, in San Diego, she partnered with the Salk Institute for Biological Studies, carrying out ground-breaking experiments linking brain function and biotechnology. Churchland is a pioneer in bridging philosophy and neuroscience; until then, most thinkers working on the self, identity or the relationship between mind and body had little interaction with the sciences. As Churchland explains: "With a few notable exceptions, contemporary moral philosophers reject outright the idea that biology has anything to teach us about the nature of human morality."[3]

Mind and Body

Neurophilosophy is a contemporary attempt to address one of the recurring questions of philosophy down the ages: the relationship between the mind and the body, an area some thinkers have identified as the soul, that imaginary entity which outlives our corporeal being, an idea Socrates pondered shortly before his death.[4] In short, neurophilosophy can help us understand who we think we are.

For example, let's say an accident or traumatic event causes amnesia and we can no longer remember anything about who we are: Our brain is the same, but have we now become another person? Equally, as we grow older and we look back over our life, perhaps trying to make sense of it, we realize that there is no coherent pattern to our actions, that we have lived little more than a series of blended lives, and so we fall back on truisms such as "I was a different person then" or "I didn't really know what I was doing."[5]

Equally, we can imagine a future in which human organs can be recreated using 3D printers at home and that our obsession to be in peak physical condition means we have already replaced 90% of our organs. In such a scenario, where our body has effectively been replaced, are we then a different person? Discussion of these and similar topics related to free choice and personal responsibility would be complex and virtually limitless.

A discussion at one of the first seminars I attended at the University of Oxford was about Gilbert Harman's "brain in a vat" scenario.[6] A brain is submerged in a container, protected by amniotic fluid. The brain is connected by electrodes to a computer that transmits a series of stimuli and information to it. For example, during the day the brain receives images and other sensory information that makes it believe it is connected to a body and living a normal life: a regular workday followed by exercise, drinks with friends and finally a few hours before bed with the family at home. The brain doesn't realize that the data and stimuli it receives are artificial. Is what the brain has "lived" real or imaginary? The brain in a vat would never know the reality of its existence unless the computer to which it is connected transferred images of the laboratory where the experiment was taking place or somebody found a way to tell it otherwise.

Little wonder that the idea of our brains being tricked in this way has caught the imagination of writers down the ages. Homer's *The Odyssey* can be interpreted as a similar experiment carried out on Ulysses by the gods, who provoke any number of incidents to delay his return home.[7] The Biblical character of Job is a good man whose loyalty and faith are tested by every sort of calamity by Yahve and the Devil. In the end, Job is rewarded for his resilience, by which time he might be forgiven for questioning his faith.[8]

More recently, in the movie *Matrix*, humanity lives in a reality generated by machines, while the cold war novel *The Manchurian Candidate*, later adapted into a film, tells the story of how an unscrupulous and ambitious US senator supported by other powerful men has had his son's brain interfered with, along with others in his marine unit, so as to make him a hero who can then be manipulated when he is elected president. Fortunately, one of the Manchurian Candidate's colleagues uncovers the plot and shoots him as he is celebrating his win in the primaries.

Rather than falling back on conspiracy theories, some people choose to make sense of their lives by rejecting the idea of free will entirely and instead believe in destiny, adopting a fatalistic approach whereby everything that happens to us is preordained.[9] In turn, some of us learn to accept responsibility for our actions, even when things don't turn out as we planned or hoped. There is an explanation for everything, and it is usually simpler than we think. Even things we can't verify for ourselves are explained by laws and theories such as relativity; similarly, there are rules for social behavior we can acquire.

Returning to the fundamental question at the center of philosophy is: Who we are and how do our minds, the part of us that thinks, remembers, feels, cries and laughs, relate to our bodies. All these processes are triggered by the senses: touch, sight, hearing, smell and taste. The two main currents of thought that have tried to address the question of how mind and body are connected are dualism and monism, two positions usually regarded as diametrically opposed, although there are views that combine both.

Dualism holds that the mind and the body are two distinct entities, but which can be connected. The dualist position rests on the belief that sensory experiences are very different from thought or rational analysis and that different faculties are used for their analysis.

Believers of the existence of a soul that outlives the body—a religious rather than a philosophical position—are dualists. The best-known proponent of this thesis was the French seventeenth-century philosopher René Descartes, the father of modern philosophy, who proposed applying methodical doubt about any proposition until it was analyzed in the cold light of reason. Descartes traced a clear separation between *res cogita* (the mind) and *res extensa* (the body), deducing that both were joined in a part of the body called the pineal gland, which he located in the chest.[10] He nevertheless believed there was a connection between mind and body, an idea most of us would intuitively accept, given our experience of how mood can affect our physicality and vice versa.

In contrast, Monism argues that mind and body are found in the same entity and have the same principle of action. This vision is consistent with the biological approach to morality proposed by Churchland, according to which the human brain is the engine of our thoughts and our actions as well as the recipient of all sensory experiences. In short, it is the central unit of operations of humans. As has been scientifically proven, the organs of the human species have evolved over millennia, only adopting their current form and function relatively recently. Our brain doesn't differ much in its composition from that of our ancestors who lived in caves, although social life has transformed exponentially, especially in the last twenty-five centuries. In other words, we have a brain designed to hunt and defend against predators that now has to function in a hypercomplex society with unlimited access to information and that requires interacting with people from far away.

Given the differences between dualism and monism, and taking into account the development of neuroscience, it is worth asking if there is any practical value in the more modulated versions of both options, between that of a dualist who defends the connection between mind and body, and that of a monist who understands that our sensory and mental faculties, although processed in the brain, belong respectively to different orders or categories. Cognitive psychologists like Daniel Kahneman argue that there are two systems of thought, one fast and instinctive, almost reflexive, and another that requires more processing time. We can answer the question "what is two plus two?" without thinking, while 24×17 will typically require some thought.[11] Kahneman's approach is similar to Plato's analogy of how our mind is like a charioteer attempting to control two horses, one impetuous and fast—our instincts and passions—and another, more leisurely and calm, which balances impulse and corrects direction.[12]

The Brain Is Our Center of Operations

Churchland defines her philosophy as "the biological approach to morality" in that "it leads us to a plausible way of understanding why we can be motivated to behave morally at all, why acting kindly or generously does not go against our nature, and why virtuous habits are valuable."[13]

For Churchland, what fundamentally distinguishes humans from other mammals, from a biological point of view, is our brain. Specifically, the evolution of the cerebral cortex, the upper part divided into two hemispheres with its familiar bulges and furrows. Relative to our size, our cortex is much larger than that of other mammals, with an average of 86 billion neurons compared to a chimpanzee's 6.5 billion. Churchland explains that if we had more neurons, our capabilities would increase exponentially. Since each neuron makes 10,000 connections or synapses, if we had ten times more neurons, our intellectual and reasoning abilities would be increased by 10 to the power of 10. By the way, every billion neurons need an average consumption of six calories a day to be able to perform properly, which adds up to 516 calories a day, which explains why we don't perform so well when we're hungry.

We humans use our neuronal capacity throughout our lives, producing synapses as a result of learning, experience or the association of ideas and knowledge. Other mammals use their neuronal capacity for finding food, defending themselves and reproducing. That explains why mammals such as bison walk from birth and soon learn to feed themselves. As we know, human babies are dependent on their parents up to relatively advanced ages compared to other species, during which time they develop greater intellectual capacity.

In light of this marvel of evolution, we can only wonder if the brains of those who succeed us over the centuries will develop an intellectual capacity we can only imagine. But as things stand, it seems more likely that artificial intelligence and machine learning will evolve much faster than the brain and perhaps develop into a more skilled species than human beings themselves.

Is it possible to increase our neuronal capacity and therefore human intelligence? In her 2019 book, *Conscience: The Origins of Moral Intuition*, Churchland discusses several aspects of typical mammal behavior as well as laboratory experiments to measure how mammal brains react to certain situations, for example, the behavior of prairie and montane voles after giving birth. Prairie voles, which are more sociable, secrete two hormones, oxytocin and vasopressin, which encouraged protective and caring behavior toward their young. Montane voles, which abandon their young after giving birth, do not secrete oxytocin or vasopressin. When scientists injected these hormones into several female montane voles, they found that they began to behave like their prairie peers, showing more care and protection toward their young. They also did the same with male prairie and montane voles, both of which normally ignored their offspring, producing greater attachment to their young.

For Churchland, experiments such as these are proof of the direct relationship between hormones, neuroreceptors and behavior. Similar experiments on humans have produced similar results. In short, it seems there is a neurobiological reality of consciousness whereby different hormones secrete substances that make us feel pain when rejected, joy in belonging to a group or the ability to feel shame and the meaning of reputation, along with self-restraint. Our conscience and sense of morality have a biological basis. As Churchland explains, "Moral norms emerge in the context of social tension, and they are anchored by the biological substrate. Learning social practices relies on the brain's system of positive and negative reward, but also on the brain's capacity for problem solving."[14]

Neuronal interaction helps us learn from experience, the association of memories, sensations and knowledge, says Churchland: "Once learned, social norms become part of a person's ever-developing extended neural network, in cortex as well as in subcortical structures. Memories, language, and imagination, along with bonding to family, friends, and tribe, will modulate and sculpt that neural network."[15]

Could Psychopharmacology Generate More Talent and Make Better Companies?

As Churchland has shown, our sense of attachment to a family or community is powerful and has a biological basis in neuroreceptor hormones such as oxytocin and vasopressin. There are many possible applications for this in management. I am particularly interested in the way employees feel about their company and whether it is possible to cultivate a feeling of attachment to an organization through the use of psychopharmacology, the scientific study of the effects that drugs have on mood, sensation, thinking and behavior.

One reason for using psychopharmacology in this way is that attracting and retaining the best talent is the main concern of human resource managers and increasingly of the CEO. Cultivating a sense of belonging to an organization encourages the best talent to continue being part of it.

Another is because as in other smaller communities such as the family, the sense of belonging to a company arouses a killer instinct to protect the values and products of the organization. For example, PepsiCo executives do not drink Coca-Cola (at least in public) and vice versa. In addition, as anthropology teaches us, a sense of belonging also awakens a killer instinct toward competitors, particularly in highly competitive sectors and even more now that trade wars across continents are back in fashion.

Finally, the same sense of belonging encourages members of the organization to attract talent. The sense of identification with an organization often has a proselytizing effect, helping to attract those we consider best, as happens within families: We want the best partners for our children.

If there is a biological basis to the sense of identification and belonging explained by Churchland and other neurobiologists, what initiatives are open to senior management to foster this feeling among the workforce?

The first, and perhaps the most obvious, is to create an organizational culture based on the most popular products and services and led by a management team with strong leadership. Neurobiology teaches us that the families and tribes able to attract and retain members are the winners, the most proactive, those that develop the strongest bonds between their members. In contrast, the losers, the isolated and those excluded from the group usually generate rejection, and this too has a biological basis.

The second is what we might call bio-improvement through the use of psychopharmacology. We might usefully ask if taking hormones such as oxytocin and vasopressin would necessarily make us more ethical. Imagine that within a few years, these hormones were available with no side effects. Would you take them? Presumably, only if you already felt a strong sense of identification with your company. At the same time, if this medication was available to everyone, it would cease to offer a competitive advantage, but at least, we would all go to work happier.

Now imagine that instead of a popular and affordable drug, a reputed company offers a unique, one-year treatment at a high price to cultivate these hormones in the body, developing sociability, empathy and a sense of belonging and of course without any side effects. Your company, a leader in its sector and with a consolidated reputation, wants to provide its managers with the best preparation for professional success, in addition to keeping them motivated, and so decides to provide you all with this treatment. Would you accept this generous offer of self-improvement?

If there were no health risks, why would you refuse? The end is good, as are the means. That said, some people might object on the basis that the treatment might alter their personality. Yet we know that hormone treatment is widespread. Many of us take melatonin, a hormone that helps us relax and sleep better. Many women take estrogen during and after menopause, and there are testosterone treatments to strengthen hair growth. There are any number of drugs that impact on our hormones.

The potential of psychopharmacology is fascinating and could have transformative effects on our body and our mind. If, as we saw earlier, our brain is not going to evolve organically to keep up with technological and social change, why not resort to chemistry to make us more sociable and experience greater happiness? As has happened before, reality will likely outdo fiction. Any number of science-fictional novels are set in future worlds where the advancement of biology, medicine and pharmacology allows us to live forever, as well as creating the conditions for a fairer, more empathic, happier society.

The third initiative is through education and lifelong learning. As we have seen, the bad news is that our brain has many physical and biological limitations; the good news is that it is also amazingly flexible and can generate new neurons over time. Some experiments have shown that study, intensive exercise of our intellectual faculties can facilitate the growth of neurons.[16]

In addition, learning, acquiring new knowledge and developing new skills keep our brains active and generate many more connections between our neurons. I have found that returning to my business school to develop a new course is like going to a brain gym. We all need to do it from time to time if we want to keep our mind in shape, in the same way we do with our bodies.

A teaching method that has highly effective results precisely because of how our brains are configured is the case method, typically used in business and law schools. As Churchland explains: "In human choice generally, behavioral and brain-imaging studies indicate that similar neural operations are involved. For example, humans, like other mammals, recognize a relevant similarity between the case at hand and other cases encountered sometime earlier in life. Psychologists call this case-based reasoning. Since we use case-based reasoning for many problems in the physical world, it is highly probable that we use it in the social world, and this conclusion is confirmed by behavioral research."[17]

At IE Business School, we know from experience that education and learning in adulthood have a decisive impact on the brain's development. A few years ago, we launched a Master in Positive Leadership and Strategy at IE University, the main purpose of which is not so much the acquisition of management knowledge, but instead to develop attitudes and habits to improve participants' quality of life. Its theoretical foundations are positive psychology, which emphasizes the importance of practicing certain virtues and habits to improve professional skills and well-being and ultimately to provide greater happiness.

In *Conscience*, Churchland reviews the conventional propositions of moral philosophy, discarding both Kantian ethics and utilitarianism, which as she points out, have nothing to do with the functioning of the brain. That said, she does subscribe to the Aristotelian philosophy of virtue proposed by some of the philosophers in this book such as Iris Murdoch, G. E. M. Anscombe or Philippa Foot. "Aristotle and Confucius stressed the importance of developing strong social habits, also known as the virtues: prudence, compassion, patience, honesty, courage, kindness, hard work, and generosity. All habits reduce the costs of decision-making. As we have seen, brains aim to keep their energetic costs as low as is consistent with well-being, and habits are one good solution to energetic efficiency (…)In other words, if you have a habit of being kind to everyone, you do not have to use time and energy figuring out what to do in a routine occasion."[18]

If we want to understand the connection between our body and our mind, perhaps the central question in philosophy, then we need to understand how the brain works at the chemical level. The importance of this organ cannot be overstated: When the brain is damaged to the point it no longer functions, even if other organs such as the heart continue to work, we are considered dead.

The problem our cerebral North Pole presents us with is that we still know very little about its sophisticated structure and much less how we generate neurons. Perhaps the US philosopher Thomas Nagel is right when he says that we must simply accept that the connection between mind and body cannot be understood at present and that a paradigm shift is required to allow us to further explore and evince phenomena that today are still unfathomable.[19]

Takeaways

Neurophilosophy is a promising area to explain the rationale behind human behavior, linking biology with morality.

- Philosophers have long focused their attention on the relationship between the mind and the body. Dualism argues that mind and body are separate entities, although as Descartes explained, they could be joined

in some part of the body. Monism, on the other hand, argues that mind and boy are wedded and that when the body dies, so does the mind. From a practical reasoning perspective, there need not be much difference between modulated versions of both approaches.
- Churchland's philosophy takes a biological approach to morality, and its aim is to demonstrate that acting in accordance with morality and living a virtuous life are consistent with our physical nature. Based on experiments with different animals, as well as research into the human brain, Churchland concludes that there is a direct relationship between hormonal activity, neuroreceptors and our conscience.
- Given that our moods and our behavior depend on the biological composition of our brain, and backing the evidence, we can identify four ways we could develop positive neuronal activity: by creating winning strategies in companies; by consuming certain amounts of psychopharmaceuticals; lifelong learning; and practicing the virtues.

Notes

1. All quotes in this section follow an interview between Belinda Holdsworth and the author on August 14, 2019.
2. Developed by Alan Turing, a British computer scientist considered as the father of artificial intelligence, the Turing Test is a test of a machine's ability to exhibit intelligent behavior. If a person who interacts with the machine cannot reliably distinguish its responses from those of a human, then the machine has passed the test.
3. P. Churchland, *Conscience: The Origins of Moral Intuition* (New York and London: W. W. Norton, 2019), p. 149.
4. In Plato, *Phaedo* (Oxford: Oxford University Press, 1995).
5. Derek Parfitt, a British philosopher who passed away in 2017, speculated about similar personal identity challenges in this book *Reasons and Persons* (Oxford: Clarendon Press and Oxford University Press, 1984).
6. Gilbert Harman, an American philosopher who retired from Princeton in 2017, has written and became a reference on epistemology, mind, relativism and knowledge. See his book with Judith Jarvis Thomson, *Moral Relativism and Moral Objectivity* (Great Debates in Philosophy) (Oxford: Basil Blackwell, 1995).
7. Homer, *The Odyssey*, Dominic Rieu et al. (London: Penguin Classics, 2003).
8. Stephen Mitchell (ed.), *The Book of Job* (New York, NY: Harper Collins, 1994).

9. See the interesting article that reviews books on conspiracy theories: J. Lepore, Taking History Personally, *Times Literary Supplement*, August 6, 2019.
10. R. Descartes, *Meditations, and Other Metaphysical Writings*, Desmond M. Clarke (trans.) (London: Penguin Classics, 1998).
11. D. Kahnemann, *Thinking, Fast and Slow* (London and New York: Penguin, 2013).
12. Plato, *Phaedrus* (Cambridge: Cambridge University Press, 2011).
13. P. Churchland, *Conscience*, op.cit., p. 169.
14. Ibid., p. 170.
15. Ibid., p. 176.
16. For example, E. Fuchs and G. Flugge, Adult Neuroplasticity: More than 40 Years of Research, *Neural Plasticity*, May 14, 2014 (541870).
17. P. Churchland, *Conscience*, op.cit., p. 16.
18. Ibid., p. 168.
19. T. Nagel, *Mortal Questions* (Cambridge: Cambridge University Press, 1991); Chapter 10: *Ethics Without Biology*.

3

Courage: Ayn Rand/Jiang Qiong Er

Ying and Yang, Tradition and Modernity: Jiang Qiong Er[1]

"Women hold up half the sky," declared Chairman Mao Zedong as he unleashed the Cultural Revolution,[2] a chaotic and violent episode in Chinese history that lasted from 1966 to 1976. His message was that women were now required to play their part in the Communist Party's drive for economic growth and should leave their traditional place in the home to join men in the factories and offices. The message was heard and probably explains why China has a higher percentage of women in the labor market than other developed nations: 61%, compared to 56% in the United States, or 55% in Germany.[3] A 2019 report by IE University's China Center shows that 25% of start-ups in China were founded by women, compared to 18% in Europe.[4]

The Cultural Revolution is rarely mentioned in modern China, and I have heard Communist Party officials and businesspeople refer to it in private as an involution rather than a revolution, even if it did achieve greater inclusion in the workplace.

I first met Jiang Qiong Er online during a case study on my corporate strategy course of the business she had started, Shang Xia, a strategic alliance with global luxury brand Hermés. I had picked this case for two reasons. Firstly, because it focuses on a Chinese company positioned within the premium and luxury industry, which for many westerners may sound counterintuitive, given the association in many people's minds of China as a source of low-cost, low-quality products. Secondly, because the case featured a very interesting protagonist, a woman who represents a link between East and West, tradition and modernity, emotions and rationality. Qiong Er's spirit of entrepreneurship empowered her to co-create a joint venture with a centennial family-run corporation with a global presence. She describes Shang Xia's mission as using "the best craft techniques and knowledge bequeathed by our ancestors as an inspiration and transforming it into contemporary forms, connecting one generation to another."

My second meeting with Qiong Er was in person at her flagship store in Shanghai, where she shared with my team her business strategy in an exquisitely decorated room over a cup of pu'er tea. Shang Xia's shop echoes Hermes' elegant style, but also evokes the sophistication of the finest Chinese craftsmanship.

Qiong Er is polite, affable and sophisticated; it's a pleasure to hear her explain the culture behind her business, and how her products blend modernity and superb manufacturing with the ancestral traditions of China. Among the products that impressed me most were an eggshell porcelain coffee set, elegant, simple and functional, light but resistant, and a hand-made, seamless woman's cashmere felt coat, pieces that you fall in love with at first sight.

Qiong Er inherited her passion for traditional Chinese culture and art from her father, Xing Tonghe, the architect who oversaw the renovation of Shanghai's Bund, the waterfront area built in the nineteenth century and early twentieth century, as well as designing the Shanghai Museum, whose form, in the shape of the traditional *ding* cooking pot, celebrates Chinese culture. Her grandfather, Jiang Xuan Yi, was a well-known artist who combined western and oriental traditions and whose paintings and etchings hang in several galleries and are rarely seen at western auction houses.

Qiong Er feels a clear link with her grandfather, who combined western art techniques with traditional Chinese landscapes. Her company is part of this legacy and has a global outlook while applying the highest Chinese standards. Shang Xia acquires its products from artisans that Qiong Er and her team have located in different areas of China, establishing long-term agreements, financing traditional production methods to guarantee manufacturing processes that create unique items and that require time and resources. Shang Xia has shops in Shanghai, as well as a center where it organizes cultural activities. There is also an outlet in Paris and plans to expand to other cities in China in the coming years. The pioneering strategy of Shang Xia in coupling traditional Chinese culture with the global premium products sector will very likely be followed by other western conglomerates soon.

Qiong Er explains the strategy behind teaming up with Hermès as combining local roots in China with a vocation for international growth, relating tradition and modernity, west with east, past and present, passion and business savvy. She is a fascinating speaker, with the care for the language and analytical mindset common among the cultivated Chinese, and with a multi-dimensional rationale that requires close attention. She explains that the name Shang Xia means above and below, following Taoist tradition, whose ideas are often the result of seemingly opposed concepts, such as Ying and Yang, but that create balance. It brings to mind Christine Gross-Loh and Michael Puett's book *The Path*: "The truth is that many Chinese philosophers actually saw the world very differently: as consisting of an endless series of fragmented, messy encounters."[5]

This equilibrium between two opposites, reason and emotion, is what Qiong Er strives for in leading her company, inculcating in her workforce a devotion for traditional know-how and craftsmanship combined with an orientation toward contemporary tastes and design. "At Shang Xia, we believe in bequeathing our heritage from one generation to the next, respecting Chinese culture in the process."

> When we think about design, we have to consider rationality, function, comfort, and wellbeing, among other elements. On top of that, we ask ourselves what makes an object valuable. We believe that emotion is what makes an object valuable.

The choice of name for her company was deliberate, and the meaning of the words has deep roots. Qiong cites two expressions as defining its value proposals. In classical Chinese, "寄情于物" (jì qíng yú wù) means "to put inner feelings into objects," in line with the company's mission, which converts the emotions of the artists or designers of the products.

At the same time, from the customer's perspective, who use Shang Xia products, comes the second phrase in classical Chinese: 情由物生 (qíng yóu wù shēng), which means "feelings that have been caused by the objects." Qiong Er believes that the feeling the artists have put into making the objects is transferred to the customers, which are then transmitted down to subsequent generations.

> We want to create objects with our emotions and then those emotions are transmitted to the customer, and our objects become treasures that can be passed on to the next generation.

Her management style is also very different to those in the west: "It's not about creating thousands of rules to manage the team; I think it's more about inspiring the team. When you inspire people, they manage themselves. Of course, it's a balance: we have basic management rules, but I believe it's more about inspiring the team."

When I ask Qiong Er about the changes required to improve diversity and inclusion in business and society, her reply reflects a much slower concept of time than is usual in the west, of a belief that social change should come about slowly, progressively, rather than abruptly, a view I have heard expressed often in China. Her thoughts on social change and time are almost metaphysical: "I do not believe we can change the society we live in, but we can be the master of our own lives. This means that we should work more on ourselves than try to change the world or complain about the system we live under. We live in a world of three dimensions, but we should never forget the fourth dimension. The fourth dimension is about time. If we only live in the three dimensions, we may try to change what we find unfair, or lacking in some way, but we should go beyond the three-dimensional mindset and include the fourth dimension."

Reflecting on her belief for the need for balance, Qiong Er believes we need to see our lives in the broader context of history, which moves at a much slower pace than our own lives.

> Our lives move forward quickly, so while change may take place over time, we rarely experience it personally. For this reason, I believe we should focus more on ourselves, on what we, as women, can do; we can master many things. We don't need to depend on others and can instead rely on ourselves. Globalization means we are now free to create value for society and to do lots of things that we could never do before. But that will only happen by focusing more on what's inside us, rather than on the world outside. Let's see what we can do, what we can do with what we have, with the time we have, the energy we have, the knowledge we have. I believe this is how we could change things.

This sense of how Chinese society changes over time as the result of personal transformation, and how this internal movement is projected as part of the whole, defines the entrepreneurial talent of Qiong Er, as well as the disruptive courage of Ayn Rand, the philosopher under discussion in this chapter. Perhaps the biggest difference between Qiong Er's entrepreneurialism and Ayn Rand is that the former sees the entrepreneur as integral to the community, forming part of it and contributing to its development from within. Rand's conception of entrepreneurs is different: She sees them as outliers, figures who are in conflict with the conventions of society, almost as revolutionaries.

Qiong Er's vision matches the Confucian idea of personal transformation and its relationship with society. To quote *The Path*: "Confucius's ideas focus on overcoming the self through ritual cultivation. He emphasizes the capriciousness of the world, which is why he also encourages us to remember the deep joy that can come from the work of building extraordinary communities at all levels, from those immediately around us to the world at large."[6]

Qiong Er and Ayn Rand share a number of traits. Rand, like Qiong, was entrepreneurial in spirit, and she, too, was an innovator. Rand too, lived under communism, but while Rand emigrated to the United States to escape Bolshevik Russia, Qiong Er, taking a longer view of history, is working to recover traditional Chinese skills and to build bridges between her country and the rest of the world. What's more, like Qiong, Rand was passionate about what she did, transferring her energy into changing the future through the present.

My encounters with artists have always stayed with me, a combination of fascination and mystery. These are the same feelings I experienced during my conversations with Qiong Er, enigmatic and with an attractive air of mystery. She brings to mind General de Gaulle's phrase: "the essence of prestige is mystery."[7]

Ayn Rand, a Conservative Thinker?

Described by veteran US political commentator Robert Reich in the context of Donald Trump's presidency as: "The intellectual godmother of modern-day American conservatism,"[8] Ayn Rand was undoubtedly an inspiration for libertarianism and a leading advocate within philosophy of the virtue of moral selfishness. As with other thinkers in this book, Rand was not recognized by many as a philosopher so much as a writer and a disseminator of ideas, partly because she was not part of the academic world, even though she spoke at many of the most prestigious universities in the United States such as Harvard or MIT, and her ideas have been studied by a growing number of researchers.

As I have argued in other parts of this book, I don't believe that philosophy is an academic closed shop: A significant number of renowned modern female thinkers never taught at universities, perhaps for reasons discussed in the introduction.

Rand's work is perhaps best understood in the context of her origins and career: "My personal life is a postscript to my works/novels: it consists of the sentence: 'And I mean it.'"[9]

Born into a Jewish Russian family, Rand lived through the Russian Revolution as a student in Saint Petersburg. She developed a passion for literature early in life, writing novels and screenplays that highlighted the role of reason, while embracing atheism. The violence of the Russian Revolution, the confiscation of her family's property, the egalitarian aims of the new regime and the pre-eminence of the collective led her to reject the idea of the common good and to defend capitalism, individualism and private property.

After graduating, Rand was given permission to visit family in the United States. Arriving in New York at the height of the roaring twenties, Rand was immediately captivated by the city's architecture, the force of this new economic power and the dynamism of its society. Having decided she wanted to be a screenplay writer, she moved to Hollywood where she met a young actor, Frank O'Connor, who she soon married.

After becoming a US citizen, her career reached its peak with the success of *The Fountainhead* in 1943,[10] a novel that tells the story of Howard Roark, a pioneering architect determined to stick to his principles, even at the cost of social and professional rejection. He ends up blowing up the building he designed because the constructor does not respect his project, but the novel has a happy ending: Roark achieves his dreams and marries the woman he loves and who shares his vision. The Fountainhead is one of the works libertarians like to cite, based on the values held by its protagonist. The film version directed by King Vidor and starring Gary Cooper and Patricia Neal has since become a classic, although Rand repudiated it.

Her second major novel, *Atlas Shrugged*,[11] published in 1957, is set in a dystopia where business leaders decide to go on strike. The protagonist, John Galt, is a firm believer in Rand's own philosophy, objectivism and who, during a lengthy speech, explains that US society is divided into two main groups: the doers, composed of the business class, and the non-doers, who are the representatives of government and religion. The figure of Atlas represents the former, who carry the weight of the world on their shoulders, creating wealth and social transformation.

Rand explained in *The Goal of My Writing*: "This is the motive and purpose of my writing: the projection of an ideal man. The portrayal of a moral ideal, as my ultimate literary goal, as an end in itself—to which any didactic, intellectual or philosophical values contained in a novel are only the means."[12]

Building on her success, Rand surrounded herself with acolytes and created an institute named after herself in order to promote her theories of objectivism. She was also a supporter of the Republican Party and several anti-communist causes. She kept a hectic schedule, attending conferences and meeting until the final years of her life. But a lifetime of smoking two packets of cigarettes a day took its toll and she eventually succumbed to cancer of the lungs, prompting one of team to sign her up to Medicare—an irony not lost on her critics. She died of a heart attack at her New York apartment. A group of admirers arranged for a wreath measuring almost two meters in the shape of a dollar for her funeral.

Rand was nothing if not contradictory: She opposed the Vietnam War, but supported Israel in the Yom Kippur War, comparing Israeli soldiers to the Europeans who eradicated the native peoples of the Americas to colonize what would become the United States. She defended abortion rights but condemned homosexuality. She had an affair with Nathanial Brandon, her disciple who set up the *Objectivity Institute*, later accusing him of behaving irrationally after he had an affair with an actress. He would later question his teacher and highlight her repressive control.

Her list of followers grows within the Republican Party. Alan Greenspan, the former Chairman of the US Federal Reserve, attended Rand's talks as a young man, citing her as having had a major impact on his thinking. US President Donald Trump, along with Paul Ryan, Speak of the House of Representatives, and Mike Pompeo, Secretary of State, also claim her as a decisive influence. Within business, Uber founder Travis Kalanick and Wikipedia creator Jimmy Wales are devotees, with Wales calling himself a believer in objectivism. Economists such as George Reisman and Ludwig Von Mises, the father of the Austrian School, supported her ideas, with the latter describing her intriguingly as "the most courageous man in America."[13]

Rand has also been claimed by the libertarians. The term was conceived and used initially among anarchists and utopian socialists, who put forward models for societies where all authority would give way to cooperatives and mutual support.

But its current meaning developed during the 1950s after a group of Republican thinkers rejected the term liberal, which had originally been associated with free-market models, arguing that Roosevelt's New Deal of the 1930s had hijacked the concept, giving it left-leaning connotations.

Central to libertarianism is the defense of personal freedom as a fundamental to social order, including freedom of choice regarding education, health and pensions and of course private property. It owes its place in modern thinking to seventeenth-century British philosopher John Locke, but its most recent exponents are to be found in the Chicago School, and notably Milton Friedman, whose dictum, "There is one and only one social responsibility of business — to increase its profits,"[14] was once taught to managers by business schools everywhere, but is now questioned or expanded to include ethical principles.

The statement published in early 2019 by the US Business Roundtable is worth noting in this regard. The body, which is made up of more than 200 leading companies, proposes a new framework of accountability for companies, in which shareholders alongside stakeholders, customers, workers, suppliers and communities. Such a move would have been considered borderline socialism not just by Rand, but by the business community until recently.

It's hardly surprising that Rand's philosophy and the characters in her novels have captured the imagination of businesspeople over the decades: She once wrote, "Since man acts among and deals with other men, I had to present the kind of social system that makes it possible for ideal men to exist and to function—a free, productive, rational system which demands and rewards the best in every man, and which is, obviously, laissez-faire capitalism."[15]

Rand described libertarians as "right-wing hippies,"[16] rejecting their ideas as well as accusing them of having stolen many of the principles of her philosophy, objectivism. Many of the basic tenets of libertarianism, at least in its most radical form, can be found in Rand's writing, as noted by Leonard Peikoff, one of her most loyal followers and who has arguably done most to keep the flame of objectivism alive.[17] Libertarianism argues for the role of the state to be reduced to its most minimally efficient: defense; conflict resolution and the guarantee of basic freedoms; and private property. Rand rejects the use of force by the state against the individual, arguing that it is irrational: "Morality ends where the gun begins."[18]

Similarly, she saw atheism as the antidote to the irrationality of religion: "Religious abstractions are the product of man's mind, not of supernatural revelation" says the hero of *The Fountainhead*.[19] She also rejected altruism and the welfare state, arguing they simply encourage dependence and laziness. For Rand, selfishness is the motor that drives wealth creation, which in turn generates autonomy and provides the individual with more options.

The essence of objectivism, said Rand, is: "the concept of man as a heroic being, with his own happiness as the moral purpose of his life, with productive achievement as his noblest activity, and reason as his only absolute."[20]

Creators as Leaders

As mentioned in the prologue to the book, I believe that management is philosophy in action: All management theories are rooted in philosophy. This view was shared by Rand, as she explained in an address at West Point entitled *Philosophy, who needs it*: "Without abstract concepts you wouldn't be able to deal with concrete, specific problems in real life (...) A philosophical system is an integrated vision of existence."[21]

The same applies to management models: They can all be traced back to a school of thought. The leadership theories that I have described as "post-modern"[22] in another of my books owe a debt to Friedrich Nietzsche, the nineteenth-century German philosopher who identified two kinds of morality, that of the master and that of the slave. The first applies to the people who lead society, those who create their own value systems. The morality of slaves applies to the rest of society's mortals and sees the behavior of the masters. But for Nietzsche, the masters are "beyond good and bad" and are subject only to their own rules, which are different to those the herd must follow. As Nietzsche points out: "To give style to one's character -- a great and rare art! He practices it who surveys all that his nature presents in strength and weakness and then molds it to an artistic plan until everything appears as art and reason, and even the weakness delights the eye...It will be the strong, imperious natures which experience their subtlest joy in exercising such a control, in such a constraint and perfecting under their own law."[23]

Rand may have rejected Nietzsche's influence as mystical and irrational, instead identifying Aristotle as her principle guide, but the ideas of the German philosopher loom large throughout her work, describing him in *The Fountainhead* as "a poet, he projects at times (not consistently) a magnificent feeling for man's greatness, expressed in emotional, not intellectual, terms."[24]

Rand argued that people can be divided into two main types: creators and parasites. Creators are independent thinkers who do not rely on others; they are productive because they create material value for society. Parasites are essentially secondhand people who create no value because they simply carried along by society.

Peikoff writes: "Nothing is given to man on Earth. Everything he needs has to be produced. And here, man faces his basic alternative: he can only survive in one of two ways: either through the independent work of his own mind or as a parasite fed by the minds of others. The creator originates.

The parasite borrows. The creator confronts nature alone. The parasite faces nature through an intermediary. The concern of the creator is the conquest of nature. The concern of the parasite is the conquest of men."[25]

Rand's creator is personified by the hero of *The Fountainhead*, who she described in her notebooks in the following terms:

> Howard Roark—The noble soul par excellence. The man as man should be. The self-sufficient, self-confident, the end of ends, the reason unto himself, the joy of living personified. Above all—the man who lives for himself, as living for oneself should be understood. And who triumphs completely(…) A quick, sharp mind, courageous and not afraid to be hurt (…) He does not suffer, because he does not believe in suffering. Defeat or disappointment are merely a part of the battle.(…) He will be himself at any cost—the only thing he really wants of life. He is in conflict with the world in every possible way- and at complete peace with himself. And his chief difference from the rest of the world is that he was born without the ability to consider others.[26]

The novels of Ayn Rand are appealing because they feature a cast of characters with extreme personalities. Her heroes possess superlative intelligence and unshakable self-confidence. They are admired and envied by the parasites, who live off them: The parasites in her books are riddled with defects and tend to come to a bad end, as typified by Wynand, Roarke's opposite in *The Fountainhead*, the owner of the newspaper who initially supports the hero but then betrays him. His punishment is to lose his wife to Roarke and then to commit suicide.

Rand's heroes seem to exist outside the world, free, original and independent. Her villains are detestable, and we are invited to reject them. At the same time, as readers, we know that reality is more complex. It's hard to imagine that anybody, whether in business, politics or the arts, could possibly be so egotistical and successful at the same time. Modern leadership theories play down charisma and instead highlight virtues such as empathy and compassion as essential to managing people.[27]

At the same time, leaders, like all of us, are a combination of creator and parasite. The bipolarity Rand subjects people to, of being in one or the other category, is unrealistic. Nobody is perfect, nobody ever achieves all their goals and the creator is thus either a hypocrite or permanently frustrated, thus failing to fulfill the imperative to be proud.

I would argue that authentic leaders have something of the creator about them—as well as the parasite, a trait that Peikoff makes veiled reference to when he explains that creators often "recreate" others' ideas, although he fails to fully explain this.[28]

In reality, Rand created a cast of characters in order to construct a moral philosophy and create aspirational models that serve as a guide for our personal lives, even if we aren't able to follow them to the letter. By the same token, even if we identify with the fundamentals of utilitarianism, deontology or moral virtue in the real world, we tend to combine ideas taken from the three main theories, which are addressed throughout this book.

Perhaps Rand's main contribution is to strip the superiority instinct of businesspeople of any complex they might have felt in the past. True leaders have a very high opinion of themselves and don't need society's approval in order to act. This independence of thought and their ability to act alone makes them into true creators. Part of the creator's identity is pride, which confirms the belief that he or she is heading in the right direction. In contrast, Rand's view is that humility is rooted in the guilt associated with the idea of original sin and incompatible with virtue.

Libertarians, among them Rand, encouraged defenders of the faith and moral selfishness to come out of the closet and feel no shame in building a public discourse in defense of the moral superiority of the creators. As Peikoff explains, "In our culture, all the moral exigencies of intelligence are ferociously attacked. Rationality is punished for being merciless, intellectuality for being sterile, selfishness for being exploitative, independence as antisocial, integrity for being rigid, honesty as impractical, justice for being cruel and productivity as materialist."[29]

It's not hard to see the connection between this narrative and some forms of supremacist popularity that periodically take root in developed countries. In contrast with Rand's model, which some people have mistakenly considered the epitome of what a business leader should be, the managers and directors running large companies are assuming greater and greater corporate social responsibility. This is the age of committed capitalism, a time when businesses are carrying out a key role in the global society and business leaders and directors are aware of the social impact of their activities and the need to build sustainable organizations. They do not operate, as Rand portrayed her creators, as though they lived on a desert island.

Another of Rand's contributions is her emphasis on the role of businesspeople in social development. Peikoff explains: "Rand's stated goal for writing the novel (*Atlas Shrugged*) was 'to show how desperately the world needs prime movers and how viciously it treats them' and to portray 'what happens to the world without them,' All along the book, there is the ongoing distinction between the 'true' entrepreneurs, who seek to make profits purely by their own innovative efforts, and the false ones who benefit from government patronage and are counted among the 'looters.'"[30]

Leaders and Administrators

In some ways, management science also distinguishes between creators and parasites. What leaders really do, a well-known article written by John P. Kotter,[31] outlines two profiles in any business: managers and leaders. The former are responsible for the day-to-day running of an organization, such as planning and budgeting, task-setting and assigning resources.

In turn, leaders use their vision to create strategies, direct change and transformation in companies, motivating and guiding everybody toward a single mission.

As with Rand's creators and parasites, the reality of the business world is more complex, and Kotter himself accepts that a combination of both qualities is required to successfully lead an organization. Ideally, people in positions of responsibility should find a dynamic balance that reflects the needs of the moment. At times of growth, vision and strategic leadership are essential; at other times, control and planning are needed.

What's more, there is no single definition of what makes a good manager or leader. Kotter explains that although management seems a more rational occupation than leadership, a kind of organizational engineering, leadership shouldn't be seen as mysterious in any way and has nothing to do with charisma or other exotic personality traits. It's not an attribute of the chosen few but is instead a capacity that's been developed over time, bringing together a compendium of characteristics, including the ability to communicate effectively with stakeholders and is much more than simply managing a series of processes.

Nietzsche's idea of the superman exercised a powerful influence in US thinking in the latter half of the nineteenth century, personified by men such as J. P. Morgan, Andrew Carnegie and John D. Rockefeller, in much the same way as happened with the rise of Germany's industrialists at the same time.[32] Similarly, the ideas of Rand and other writers almost a century later were seminal in creating modern leadership theories that saw their zenith during the Reagan and Thatcher years of the 1980s and most memorably expressed as "Greed is good": Gordon Gekko's dictum in the movie Wall Street.

Peikoff summarized Rand's thinking in his book *The Philosophy of Ayn Rand* as "The direct source of current wealth was the Industrial Revolution. The cause was reason and liberty, which made possible knowledge and action, which is to say, modern science and the modern business class."[33]

Rand's spirit lives on in the new wave of entrepreneurs driving the technological disruption of the new millennium, and one can't help but compare Mark Zuckerberg or Elon Musk with the heroes of Atlas Shrugged.

Takeaways

Ayn Rand is considered one of the pillars of libertarianism, the concept of political philosophy that calls for minimal government, while defending personal freedoms such as private property, education, health and pensions.

- Rand's work typically features model entrepreneurs, committed to their values and free from authority. Entrepreneurs are the "doers," while those who work in the public sector or for organized religion are "parasites." Her model society is arguably more an aspiration than a reality.
- Current leadership has evolved from the post-modern ideas inspired by thinkers such as Nietzsche or Rand, whose leaders were charismatic and beyond right or wrong, toward more multi-faceted and realistic models. Today's more engaged capitalism, where leaders must increasingly respond to a range of stakeholders, means that directors need to balance their abilities as managers and leaders.

Notes

1. All quotes in this section follow an interview between Jiang Qiong Er and the author held on September 20, 2019.
2. T. Phillips, In China 'Women Hold Up Half of the Sky', but Can't Touch the Political Glass Ceiling, *The Guardian*, October 14, 2017. https://www.theguardian.com/world/2017/oct/14/in-china-women-hold-up-half-the-sky-but-cant-touch-the-political-glass-ceiling.
3. A. Qin, The Challenge of Reporting on Women in China, Where Men Control the Narrative, *New York Times*, July 18, 2019.
4. B. Ma, *Chinese vs European Entrepreneurship: A Comparison*, Report of IE University China Center, working document, October 3, 2019.
5. M. Puett and C. Gross-Loh, *The Path: What Chinese Philosophers Can Teach Us About the Good Life* (New York, NY: Simon & Schuster, 2016); Kindle ed., loc. 330.
6. M. Puett and C. Gross-Loh, Confucius, Mencius, Laozi, Zhuangzi, Xunzi: Selected Passages from the Chinese Philosophers, in *The Path*, op. cit., Kindle ed., loc. 44.
7. A. Sampson, *The Midas Touch: Money, People and Power from West to East* (London: Hodder & Stoughton, 1989); p. 34.
8. (Robert) R. Reich, Trump's Brand Is Ayn Rand, Robert Reich's Blog, March 25, 2018. http://www.smirkingchimp.com/thread/robert-reich/78017/trump-s-brand-is-ayn-rand?fb_comment_id=1615500661902238_1615626048556366.

9. A. Rand, *Atlas Shrugged* (New York, NY: Penguin, 1997); references here are made to: "La Rebelión de Atlas" (Barcelona: Planeta/CEOE, 2019); Kindle ed., loc. 27631.
10. A. Rand, *The Fountainhead* (New York, NY: Penguin, 1993); Kindle ed.
11. A. Rand, *Atlas Shrugged*, op. cit.
12. A. Rand, *The Fountainhead*, op. cit., loc. 124.
13. J. Burns, *Godless Capitalism: Ayn Rand and the American Right* (New York: Oxford University Press, 2009); p. 114. https://mises.org/library/ayn-rands-contribution-cause-freedom.
14. M. Friedman, The Social Responsibility of Business Is to Increase Its Profits, *New York Times*, September 13, 1970.
15. A. Rand, *The Fountainhead*, op. cit., p. iv.
16. P. Avrich, *Anarchist Voices: An Oral History of Anarchism in America* (Princeton, NJ: Princeton University Press); p. 6.
17. Objectivism is the name used to designate the philosophy of Ayn Rand, and its main thesis is the rational individualism outlined in her novels.
18. L. Peikoff, *Objetivismo: La Filosofía de Ayn Rand*, D. Garcia, Spanish Edition (trans.) (New York: Penguin, 2013). Kindle ed., Ch. 10., loc. 7714.
19. A. Rand, *The Fountainhead*, op. cit., p. iv.
20. A. Rand, *Atlas Shrugged*, op. cit., Kindle ed., loc. 3102.
21. A. Rand, *Philosophy: Who Needs It* (introd., L. Peikoff) (New York: Penguin, 1984); p. 5.
22. S. Iniguez de Onzono, *The Learning Curve: How Business Schools Are Reinventing Education* (London: Palgrave Macmillan, 2011); p. 26.
23. R.J. Hollingdale, *Nietzsche: The Man and His Philosophy* (Cambridge: Cambridge University Press, 1999); p. 143.
24. A. Rand, *The Fountainhead*, op. cit., Kindle ed., loc. 193.
25. L. Peikoff, *Objectivism*, op. cit., Kindle ed., loc. 6249.
26. A. Rand, *The Fountainhead*, op. cit., Kindle ed., loc. 15755.
27. See for example, J. Collins, *Good to Great: Why Some Companies Make the Lead and Others Don't* (New York, NY: Harper Collins, 2001).
28. L. Peikoff, *Objectivism*, op. cit., Kindle ed., loc. 6421.
29. Ibid., loc. 7565.
30. Ibid. loc. 6402.
31. J.P. Kotter, What Leaders Really Do, in *Harvard Business Review on Leadership* (Boston: Harvard Business Review Press, 1990); p. 38.
32. J. Ratner-Rosenhagen, *American Nietzsche: A History of an Icon and an Ideal* (Chicago: The University of Chicago Press, 2012).
33. L. Peikoff, *Objectivism*, op. cit., Kindle ed., loc. 7241.

4

Virtue: Philippa Foot/Angelica Kohlmann

Science, Business and Cosmopolitanism: Angelica Kohlmann[1]

Held each year at the Vienna Hofburg imperial palace, the Peter Drucker Forum brings together thoughtful business leaders to discuss the latest management ideas and models. This isn't an academic event, but a mix of investigators, consultants, specialist journalists, entrepreneurs and managers who discuss not simply theories, but how ideas can be put into practice to make businesses into models for social change.

The blended aspect of the Forum, of bringing together researchers and practitioners, speculation and experience, would have appealed particularly to Peter Drucker, who is rightly considered the father of modern management, and while no academic taught management at several universities and wrote many influential books and articles on the subject.[2]

The Chairman of the Drucker Forum Advisory Board and the European Peter Drucker Society that supports it is Angelica Kohlmann, a member of Drucker's wife family, who co-organizes the event with Richard Straub, its President. As Peter Drucker's birthplace, Vienna is particularly appropriate for the event—a crossroads of intellectuals, artists, writers and entrepreneurs, also birthplace of psychologists, philosophers and musicians, home to outstanding economists such as Ludwig von Mises, Friedrich Hayek or Joseph Schumpeter.

Although her family is European, Kohlmann was born in Brazil and spent her first years in São Paulo, as her parents had emigrated to Latin America.

Her personality reflects the enviable synergy between a Germanic sense of duty and discipline with the vibrancy traditionally associated with the culture of Brazil. She holds a German and a Brazilian passport. "We grew up in a very international environment, traveling a lot, with relatives in the United States, in Europe, and elsewhere across the world.

> This impacted my life. Certainly, I love Brazil, where I grew up. But I always appreciated the high cultural level I found in Europe, along with other philosophies and mindsets, and the way capitalism is understood in America. I tried to learn the best from each culture and country, and I always felt that I was a world citizen and not Brazilian or German or anything else."

As with other people who have been exposed to different cultures from a young age or who have lived in diverse countries, such as the children of diplomats or executives posted abroad, rather than identifying with a single country, Kohlmann has a more international outlook, an identity associated with global citizenship. Furthermore, she has developed an interest in a range of cultures, along with a deep-rooted respect and tolerance for human diversity in all its forms.

Research shows that children exposed to different cultures, or who show an interest in other societies, tend to have a greater capacity for leadership than those brought up in the same place and who feel tied to their domestic environment.[3] Our sense of belonging to a group is fundamentally cultural, a habit we acquire through education from infancy onward, and of course can be modified through experience and education.

Kohlmann shows a deep gratitude toward her parents for her upbringing, "which had a strong impact on how later I made my decisions.

> They gave us a broad international outlook, stressing the importance of education and, above all, they gave us self-confidence, in the sense that as long as you're honest, you work hard and you have strict ethical views, there is no limit to what you can achieve or how far you can go. I always felt a strong sense of self-confidence from my first job about what I was doing and I think this helped me a lot to move on and make decisions. Of course, this was based on a good education which I was fortunate to receive, and which is not to be taken for granted, but it was just this feeling that as long as you work hard you can go very far, and I think this was much more important than having studied medicine, for example."

This self-confidence allowed her to take on roles and make the decisions she wanted. "When I was a teenager and attended college, girls stuck together and talked about fingernails, and the young men were discussing politics. I always preferred to be with the young men, discussing politics; I understood that I wanted to be part of society." She also understood from an early age that while she wanted a family, she also wanted to develop a fulfilling career, and so set about combining them: "I knew that organizational skills were highly important.

> I needed to be able to organize the kids. I also knew that if they were sick or anything happened to them, they would come first, but as long as they were healthy and happy, then I could continue my work, and I think both aspects of my life profited from that."

Kohlmann says she has always enjoyed her relationship with her children, finding time, particularly around the table, to deepen the family experience, perhaps compensating for her absences:

> During family trips we would make, at least once a year, we spend hours at the dinner table discussing science, politics, economics, and we would have discussions deep into the night sometimes, it was a lot of fun. When they were younger I felt I was more knowledgeable, but today it's not the case. It's nice to see that I brought up kids who have so many ideas and so much input: it was a pleasure to combine my professional life with bringing up children. It was a challenge. It was a lot of work, a lot of organization. It was my choice and it was wonderful and completely doable.

Kohlmann studied medicine in Germany, although she never felt a strong vocation to be a doctor. Her real interest was in how science could impact on society. After graduating, she worked as a doctor and researcher at the Anderson Cancer Center in Houston and the Kettering Cancer Center in New York. But she found laboratory work monotonous, while treating cancer patients exposed her to deep pain and suffering. She realized that she was more oriented toward action and so decided to make the leap into the business world at a time when pharmaceutical companies were looking for professionals with a medical background that could combine their research experience with management.

She was offered a number of positions and opted to work in marketing for Behringwerke AG. Despite having no experience in the field, she was attracted to the global orientation of the post, leading a team of people and also being able to use her language skills. Over time, she was asked to work in a support capacity for the board of directors at Hoechst, which gave her a more holistic understanding of the business, analyzing investments and evaluating the financial performance of the company's different business units, a task she enjoyed, given her passion for numbers and mathematics. "I found that combining some medical knowledge with numbers was the perfect place for me in those days.

> I was 26 years old and I realized that at the board meeting there were thirty people, comprising board members and supporting staff, and I was the only woman. It took me some time to realize this, I was blind to it. I think it might have been my age or not seeing that I was different in those days that helped me a lot, I just moved on."

Since then, Kohlmann's career has advanced, as she explains, with some unexpected turns along the way, and she has continued to apply her Philosophy of generating a positive impact as she takes on greater responsibilities, even setting up her own venture fund with her children that invests in biotech, tech and related sectors. Asked about the milestones in her career, she remembers her years at the head of Behringwerke's global restructuring team, a time when she was given a free hand and that allowed her to develop a sense of responsibility and learn many aspects of management, among them taking risks and making mistakes in a relatively safe environment. Over the course of her career, Kohlmann has cultivated and strengthened a series of virtues that are fundamental for the good practice of management: discipline, dedication, determination and commitment to her ethical principles.

She still remembers her conversations with her uncle, Peter Drucker, at his home in the Rockies, when he would advise her to practice the virtue of listening, vital to leadership. She admits to not being a good listener and having largely acted independently. After reading his books, she says she now understands better the centrality of people to the practice of management. In his memoirs, Drucker refers to an episode at Cambridge University when he was attending a seminar given by John Maynard Keynes: "All the students were interested in the behavior of commodities, while for me, the behavior of people was much more interesting." Virtues and people, two central themes in the Philosophy of Philippa Foot.

Philippa Foot, Oxford and Analytical Philosophy

Summertown is a small English village that lies on the old road from Oxford to Woodstock and that over time has merged into the university city. A good number of students and teachers live in this friendly and manageably sized community, cycling to and from their schools and colleges. Summertown was also home to three of the most outstanding philosophers of the last century, gathered together in this book: G. E. M. Anscombe, Iris Murdoch and Philippa Foot. Despite their diverse political beliefs and attitudes, the three women maintained a friendship and academic exchange that reflected their shared influences: the Greek tradition of Plato and Aristotle, the scholastic rigor of St. Thomas Aquinas, Ludwig Wittgenstein and British analytical philosophy. The three were also active in raising a debate focused on the horrors of Nazism and World War II, which was a longstanding reference within the field of legal and moral Philosophy and is still seen as an example of the evil humans are capable of.

Philippa Foot grew up in a well-to-do family. Her mother was the daughter of US President Grover Cleveland and her father a businessman with steel mills in the northern county of Yorkshire. Her early education took place at home, administered by governesses, from whom she said she did not even learn "which came first, the Romans or the Greeks."[4] However, she was able to prepare to enter Oxford University's women-only Somerville College—other colleges didn't open to women until 1974—and that attracted other distinguished females students like Margaret Thatcher and Indira Gandhi. There she earned a first-class degree in Philosophy, Politics and Economics.

She was associated with Somerville throughout her academic life, working as a researcher and lecturer, although she was also a visiting professor at several US universities, notably maintaining a dual affiliation with the University of California, Los Angeles. An atheist, she also kept out of politics, although some of her books dealt with issues such as abortion or euthanasia, and she was also a government economic adviser for a short period. She was briefly married to military historian and former British military intelligence officer M. R. D. Foot and died, curiously enough, on the day of her 90th birthday.

To better understand Foot's work, we need to understand the evolution of analytical philosophy, which focuses on the study of concepts and the use of language. G. E. Moore's *Principia Ethica*[5] is usually considered the seminal work of analytical Philosophy. Its two central approaches are often defined as non-cognitivism and the distinction between metaethics and normative ethics.

In short, non-cognitivism argues that moral judgments do not respond to a true/false paradigm, because in reality there are no moral facts to refer to, contrary to scientific propositions, which can be demonstrated in relation to observable things. An early example of non-cognitivism is David Hume, the Scottish philosopher who in the eighteenth century rejected what he termed the naturalistic fallacy, which makes normative judgments based on observable truths.[6] Hume rejected the concept of human nature, seeing it as a construct elaborated by those who wanted to build a system of precepts derived merely from what they thought to be human nature. An example of this derivation of normative judgments from factual observations, for example, would be to say that because most people get married and have children, it is therefore the duty of all to marry and have children.

Moore's second proposition to try to solve the challenges of naturalistic fallacy was that we must distinguish between metaethics and normative ethics. Metaethics deals with moral concepts such as the meaning of "good," "bad" or "right," as well as how to structure moral judgments so as to be consistent. Normative ethics, on the other hand, deals with how to act in certain circumstances: for example, when it is moral to practice euthanasia. Moore explains that it is necessary first to build a good metaethical construct before moving on to normative ethics; otherwise, we make unjustified propositions that incur naturalistic fallacies.

Little wonder that so many twentieth-century philosophers spent so much time debating metaethical concepts. Foot decided to tackle non-cognitivism, among other reasons because of its distance from the kind of practical questions most of us are interested in:

> Looking back … one may be surprised and a little sad, that this particular conflict, about 'fact and value', has occupied so much of our time. We seem to have rushed on to the field without waiting to map the territory supposedly in dispute, ready to die for some thesis about commendation or approval, about pro-attitudes or evaluation before anyone had done much detailed work on the specific, and very different, concepts involved.[7]

Foot aimed to build bridges between realms, values and facts. Throughout her professional career, her views changed, but she retained her principal objective: to unravel the nature of morality, provide reasons to act morally, as well as discussing how to proceed when faced with moral dilemmas. At the end of her career, she raised a recurring question among some philosophers:

> I have been asked the very pertinent question as to where all this leaves disputes about substantial moral questions. Do I really believe that I have described a method for settling them all? The proper reply is that in a way nothing is settled, but everything is left as it was.[8]

The Meaning and Relevance of Virtue

An exponent of virtue ethics, Foot nevertheless said she felt closer to the contractualism of John Rawls or Tim Scanlon[9] (8) a school of thought that sees moral principles as the outcome of a reasonable, if hypothetical, agreement between members of society. Rawl's, which he denominates "political liberalism," "is based on the idea that political principles should not be built on any single comprehensive doctrine, but should avoid sectarianism as far as possible, while still espousing some core moral doctrines that may be able to command an 'overlapping consensus' among the holders of all the reasonable comprehensive doctrines."[10]

On the other hand, virtue ethics focuses on the character of the individual and the way our personality is reflected in our actions and decisions. This is different to consequentialism, which holds that the outcome or consequences of a particular action determine whether it is morally acceptable or not. It also differs from deontology, which argues that the rightness or wrongness of an act is determined by its nature and its adherence to and consistency with certain principles or norms. In practice, the difference between these three alternative models of morality is how problems are addressed, the way a decision is reached or justified and not necessarily the final decision reached, with which they might agree. For example, a consequentialist might argue that stealing is wrong because of the negative consequences that result from it. A deontologist might argue that theft is always wrong, regardless of any potential "good" that may come from it. However, proponents of the ethics of virtue would explain that a robbery stems from immoral behavior, as opposed to practicing the virtue of justice, which demands respect for the property of others.

With its origins in the writings of Plato and Aristotle,[11] the ethics of virtue was the predominant model in the ancient and medieval worlds. It emphasizes the character of the individual, of our conscience and will, rather than addressing rules or the consequences of our decisions. Following this classical tradition, Foot argued that there are "three essential features of a virtue — first, a virtue is a disposition of the will; second, it is beneficial either to others, or to its possessor as well as to others; third, it is corrective of some bad general human tendency."[12]

The use of the word "disposition" is interesting: Unlike "habit," which derives from Aquinas's "habitus," something that results in relatively automatic conduct, disposition suggests self-control, awareness and willingness. In any case, virtues are attributes we achieve over time through the joint exercise of reason, which decides which virtues to practice, and will, which decides the repetition of acts to acquire that disposition. They are not innate abilities and can even be cultivated later in life.

Plato was the first philosopher to analyze the main virtues, which he explored in *The Republic*,[13] summarizing them into four, associated with the different social classes of that time: Temperance, applicable to all social classes, but especially workers, a virtue aimed primarily at containing the excesses of anger and passion. Courage, associated with the military class, emphasizes the bravery and mettle soldiers require. Prudence (or wisdom) is a trait required of rulers and should guide law and leadership in society, and finally, justice lies beyond social classes and regulates the relationships between them and among the citizenry.

Foot includes these four cardinal virtues, which she considers essential for the individual's development in society, although she expands the list. All must meet the three defining requirements of the virtues outlined above, although in some cases Foot's explanations seem lacking. For example, when she talks about practicing the virtue of charity, which while making us materially poorer, strengthens our moral qualities, or when somebody who is suffering from depression gains no satisfaction from practicing virtues. Foot's approach is not focused on the practice of a particular virtue, but instead on the balanced exercise of all of them, of a system of virtues that is agreed upon by members of society.

The ethics of virtue has also influenced psychology. In its origins, psychology dealt with pathological cases, people who posed a risk to society or to themselves. However, in recent times the positive psychology movement, whose goal is to "find and nurture genius and talent" and "make normal life more fulfilling," has grown and is part of any number of personal development programs and business management. Christopher Peterson and Martin Seligman, two of the movement's best-known proponents, are the authors of *Character Strengths and Virtues*,[14] which discusses the six most important virtues for the development of a happy life. Seligman adds two virtues to the four outlined above: humanity, which has to do with the practice of altruism toward our fellow men and women; transcendence, perhaps the least personal and most elusive virtue, which refers to the impact our behavior has on the world as well as with aspects of spirituality.

It's not hard to anticipate the reception that the analysis of virtues, as reflected in good business practices, has had on the field of management. One of the objectives of business education, executive training or coaching is to develop skills that emphasize leadership or effectiveness in managerial performance, their measurement, supervision and promotion. These managerial skills are similar to virtues and even have a certain moral reach.

There is no shortage of books about the virtues required of managers. One of the best known is Stephen Covey's 1989 *The 7 Habits of Highly Effective People*,[15] which has prompted any number of sequels. Interestingly, a virtue that has largely been ignored by most philosophers, except within the Christian canon, is humility. Philippa Foot is no exception, mentioning it only in passing when she criticizes Nietzsche's concept of the superman.[16]

That said, more recent management literature does recognize the relevance of humility, seeing it as the ability that allows leaders to avoid arrogance, to listen and to be permanently oriented toward change and innovation. For example, Jim Collins, author of *From Good to Great*, proposes a model called *5 Level Leadership*, which places major emphasis on humility. Among the common factors successful companies share is that they have leaders who "build enduring greatness through a paradoxical combination of personal humility and professional will."[17] This is certainly paradoxical, given that among the most common qualities associated with business leaders, and sometimes encouraged by business schools, are a sense of superiority and belonging to an elite, typically resulting in overconfidence and even arrogance. But in Collins' view, this arrogance often prevents us from understanding and assimilating what is happening around us and acting accordingly.

The Trolley Problem and the Ethics of Artificial Intelligence

Philosophers have often used real-life cases or fictional examples, stories, metaphors, analogies and aporias to illustrate their arguments, to discuss possible choices in the face of a dilemma or to anticipate the results of a decision. These "simulators" allow thinkers explore their discourse without real risk. Plato came up with the allegory of the cave to explain the nature of human knowledge; Zeno of Elea analyzed the conceptual infinity of space by explaining that Achilles, the Greek hero admired for his agility and speed, would never be able to reach a turtle because the distance that separates them could be divided and subdivided into infinite parts, which in theory would be impossible to overcome however fast he went.[18]

Foot is also remembered for the suppositions she proposed to understand the nature of moral decisions. Some of her cases have become classics, applied and developed by other philosophers and used as a basis for debate in undergraduate programs. Perhaps the most known is the trolley problem, which she proposed in 1967[19] and that can be summarized through the following dilemma:

A runaway trolley car is moving toward five people tied to the tracks. You are standing next to a lever. If you pull the lever, the trolley will be redirected onto a side track and the five people on the main track will be saved. However, there is a single person lying on the side track who would be able to stop the tram but who would be killed in the process. Should you pull the lever?

Most people who are faced with this problem tend to be in favor of pulling the lever, seeing it as the best moral action: Rather than doing nothing, it is preferable to act to avoid greater evil. A utilitarian analysis would also justify this decision: It's five lives versus one and the comparative calculation comes out in favor of the majority. If the dilemma is posed to MBA students, the decision is taken quickly, because managers are used to solving decisions speedily and take action. In addition, Hollywood has us accustomed to the hero in action films having to intervene decisively to avoid a greater evil, whatever the consequences.

A utilitarian or a consequentialist would justify pulling the lever, since the overall result is the most satisfactory. But even for a deontologist, the obligation to always act in accordance with duty, regardless of the consequences, could also justify the decision to pull the lever, given the concurrence of the two duties of assisting somebody in danger and of avoiding involuntary manslaughter, almost in defense of others, is resolved in favor of the former.

There are variants that illustrate the complexity of solving seemingly simple dilemmas. For example, writing in the 1980s, US moral philosopher Judith Jarvis Thomson[20] posed an alternative in which the track where the one man is tied continuous in a loop, returning to the track where the five people are tied up. Would you push the button in this case? Again, most people still pull the lever, although the train will eventually run the five people over.

The supposition can even take on nuances of a qualitative or evaluative nature, not necessarily in relation to the number of people involved. Let's imagine that the five people tied to the track have been sent to prison for murder, and that the man on the alternative route is a scientist who will find a cure for cancer. Or let's say that the five tied to the track have been diagnosed with terminal diseases and at best have a year to live and the man on the other track is our scientist. What would you do?

Most philosophers who do not believe in consequentialism or utilitarianism would argue that any decision should not be made by comparing the value of one life over another. Firstly, because everyone has the right to life, regardless of their worth from an external perspective or how long they're going to live. Secondly, because that right and the other rights of the individual are a buffer against majority decisions or arguments of general interest. They act as counterweights, as guarantees against the majority deciding for the minority or the individual.[21]

The trolley problem and similar cases raised by contemporary philosophers help us understand the complexity of solving moral problems not only by human beings, but also by artificial intelligence fed by algorithms. We know that many decisions and information processes are based on algorithms. Behind every click on our computer, there is an algorithm. Algorithms are capable of making decisions on the stock markets and in daily regular business, allocating services to consumers, flying aircraft and driving cars, composing music and even writing articles, to cite just a few examples. Ed Finn, who has explored the moral dilemmas raised by the use of AI, explains: "The word algorithm frequently encompasses a range of computational processes including close surveillance of user behaviors, 'big data' aggregation of the resulting information, analytics engines that combine multiple forms of statistical calculation to parse that data, and finally a set of human-facing actions, recommendations, and interfaces that generally reflect only a small part of the cultural processing going on behind the scenes."[22]

It's predicted that within a few years, much public and private transport will be self-driven. It's worth pointing out the word automobile means self-driving. When this happens, cars and other vehicles will be guided by algorithms and will have to address Philippa Foot's Trolley dilemma, except that a machine has much better reflexes than a human being, as we have seen with aircraft automatic pilot systems, in most cases saving lives but sometimes causing tragedies.[23]

Imagine, for example, as already proposed in some university courses of philosophy and technology, that a car that traveling at a certain speed approaches a mother crossing the road outside of a zebra crossing. The car has two alternatives: run over the mother and her child, or turn sharply and run over an old man standing by the road. How should the algorithm that will decide the fairest course of action be designed?

As a number of writers have shown, the configuration of algorithms is not a morally or culturally neutral issue. Algorithms identify that data is relevant, how to interpret that data and what decision to make accordingly. Logically, in this context, the development and classification of human profiles are ongoing and necessary. Amazon, for example, tracks all its users' purchases and searches to identify their tastes and alert or advise them as to similar products and services. This has huge advantages for businesses and also for consumers, as it allows supply and demand to be balanced more effectively and cheaply.

At the same time, there is a clear risk. Profiling and categorizing people emphasizes social bias and helps to further discriminate against minorities. US academic Robert Elliott Smith, who has spent more than 30 years studying algorithms, argues in his powerful 2019 book *Rage Inside the Machine* that, "In the last few years, algorithms have been generating some surprisingly unsavory and unexpected outputs. In 2015, British daily The Guardian reported that Google algorithms tagged images of black people as '#animals', '#apes' and '#gorillas'. They also reported that Google image searches for 'unprofessional hair' predominately returned pictures of black women. 8 Another report revealed that Google's algorithms showed high-paying job ads to men more than ever than to women."[24]

At the same time, we know that the opinions and data found on social networks are often influenced by fake news, which in turn can distort machine learning. Elliott also provides an example: "When Microsoft released a Twitter bot (AI algorithm) called 'Tay' in 2016, it had to be shut down after just 24 hours because it learned to say, 'I fucking hate feminists and they should all die', 'Hitler was right I hate the Jews' and 'WE'RE GOING TO BUILD A WALL, AND MEXICO IS GOING TO PAY FOR IT' 11."[25]

Returning to the example of self-driving cars, we can imagine some of the possible problems that might occur if the algorithm behind the solution to ethical dilemmas is fed by prejudice and fake news. The same could to applications developed to make decisions in companies such as assessing the most important members of the workforce and who deserve promotion or a pay rise by using information about likely illnesses.

At the same time, there is the not-insignificant issue of the gap that might be opened between managers and other stakeholders affected by the decisions made by new technologies. Let's imagine that a downsizing is carried out based on the recommendations of a complex algorithm. Senior management can distance themselves from their decisions by saying, "it wasn't me, it was the technology." This issue has already been raised by Bernard Williams in relation to the use of technology in warfare, for example, to decide the location of bombing targets and how intense bombardments should be, even to the extent of using drones to minimize human involvement.[26] This kind of disintermediation in war makes it easier to tackle the tough decisions that were once the responsibility of senior officers.

Finally, it's tempting to wonder whether AI will eventually develop virtues through machine learning, as humans have. After all, if virtues are acquired through the repetition of acts, and machine learning also evolves, perhaps engineers will be able to program algorithms that lead to the development of virtues, thus helping us avoid the dystopias and robot dictatorships predicted by Stephen Hawking and Elon Musk.

Takeaways

Philippa Foot is an exponent of the Philosophy of virtue as a paradigm of morality, a widely accepted concept within professional development models for its direct relationship, and even conceptual identity, with managerial abilities or skills:

- The virtues are good operative habits that can be acquired through the repetition of acts, exercising intelligence and will. For many philosophers and directors, they have been a useful reference as part of personal and professional improvement.
- Philosophy has traditionally provided three main paradigms for resolving moral dilemmas: deontology, which determines how to act on the basis of applying rules and principles; consequentialism, which establishes the right or wrong of an act on the basis of its outcomes; and virtue theory, which calls on us to cultivate good habits that generate a disposition to behave with propriety. Although these three paradigms have different reasonings, they will likely lead to similar outcomes. Business leaders tend toward consequentialism, based as it is on results, as well as moral virtue.
- Foot proposes several examples and aporias that anticipate the moral dilemmas posed by artificial intelligence. As things stand, and until real progress is made in introducing moral virtue into AI algorithms, I believe it is better that moral dilemmas are resolved by people.

Notes

1. All quotes in this section follow an interview between Angelica Kohlmann and the author held on August 12, 2019.
2. S. Denning, The Best of Peter Drucker, *Forbes*, July 29, 2014. https://www.forbes.com/sites/stevedenning/2014/07/29/the-best-of-peter-drucker/#789389fa5a96.
3. H. Gardner and Emma Laskin, *Leading Minds: An Anatomy of Leadership* (New York: Basic Books, 2011); Ch. 2.
4. J. Hacker-Wright, *Philippa Foot's Moral Thought* (London and New York: Bloomsbury, 2013); p. 3.
5. G.E. Moore, *Principia Ethica* (Cambridge: Cambridge University Press, 1994).
6. D. Hume, *A Treatise of Human Nature*, L.A. Selby Bigge (ed.) (Oxford: Oxford University Press); Second edition.
7. J. Hacker-Wright, *Philippa Foot's Moral Thought*, op. cit., p. 9.

8. Ibid., p. 149.
9. John Rawls' celebrated *A Theory of Justice* (Cambridge, MA: Harvard University Press, 1971) marked a contemporary influential rebirth of contractualism. Vid. Also T. Scanlon, *What We Owe to Each Other* (Cambridge, MA: Harvard University Press, 2000).
10. M.C. Nussbaum, *The Cosmopolitan Tradition* (Cambridge, MA: Harvard University Press, 2019); p. 14.
11. Plato argues on the virtues in his dialogue *Protagoras* (Oxford: Clarendon Press, 1996) and in *The Republic* (Oxford: Oxford University Press, 2008); Aristotle deals with virtue in his *The Nicomachean Ethics*, L. Brown (ed.) (Oxford: Oxford University Press, 2009).
12. J. Hacker-Wright, *Philippa Foot's Moral Thought*, op. cit., p. 77.
13. Plato, *The Republic*, op. cit., Book 4.
14. C. Peterson and M.E.P. Seligman, *Character Strengths and Virtues: A Handbook and Classification* (Oxford and New York: Oxford University Press, 2004).
15. S.R. Covey, *The 7 Habits of Highly Influential People: Powerful Lessons in Personal Change* (New York, NY: Rosetta Books, 2013).
16. J. Hacker-Wright, *Philippa Foot's Moral Thought*, op. cit., Ch. 7.
17. J. Collins, Level 5 Leadership: The Triumph of Humility and Fierce Resolve. *Harvard Business Review* (January 2011), 67.
18. Zeno's paradoxes were described by Aristotle in *Physics*, C.D. Reeve (trans.) (Indianapolis: Hackett, 2018).
19. P. Foot, The Problem of Abortion and the Doctrine of the Double Effect, in *Virtues and Vices and Other Essays in Moral Philosophy* (Oxford: Basil Blackwell, 1978); Ch. 2.
20. J. Jarvis Thomson, Killing, Letting Die and the Trolley Problem, 59 *The Monist* (1976), 204–217 and The Trolley Problem, 94 *Yale Law Journal* (1985), 1395–1415.
21. This is supported by R. Dworkin, who conceives rights as trumps against the will of the majority: *Taking Rights Seriously: With a New Appendix, Response to Critics* (London: Bloomsbury, 1977).
22. E. Finn (ed.), *What Algorithms Want: Imagination in the Age of Computing* (Cambridge, MA: MIT Press, 2017); Kindle ed., loc. 359.
23. W. Langewiesche, What Really Brought Down the Boeing 737 Max, *The New York Times*, September 18, 2019. https://www.nytimes.com/2019/09/18/magazine/boeing-737-max-crashes.html.
24. R.E. Smith and Robert Elliott, *Rage Inside the Machine: The Prejudice of Algorithms, and How to Stop the Internet of Making Bigots of Us All* (London: Bloomsbury, 2019); Kindle ed., loc. 20.
25. Ibid.
26. B. Williams, *Mortal Questions* (Cambridge: Cambridge University Press, 1979); Ch. 5: *War and Massacre*.

5

Love: Iris Murdoch/María Benjumea

Passion Enlightens a Professional Life: María Benjumea[1]

Can you visualize a Babel of businesspeople? Imagine a vast meeting of more than 6000 entrepreneurs from all over the world, 1100 investors, venture capitalists and business angels, all gathered in huge magical space, interacting frenetically, bubbling over, explaining their ideas and interviewing each other in parallel, formal and informal meetings, a marathon of activities lasting around 72 hours.

This isn't Silicon Valley, but the South Summit, a global platform that is now a global reference point for entrepreneurship, held in Madrid every year since 2012 and the brainchild of María Benjumea, a Spanish businesswoman whose passion and enthusiasm run like electricity through meeting.

It's not easy to create the circumstances to generate such a unique entrepreneurial atmosphere, and just as hard to attract genuine creators and investors. Entrepreneurs tend to avoid formal events along the lines of Davos, instead preferring more casual, informal occasions, where interaction is direct and flows spontaneously.

As with other platform-based initiatives, the secret of South Summit's success largely lies in the capacity of somebody like Benjumea, her teams and her partners, to mobilize a network of diverse, relevant and international stakeholders, and then to leverage social networks, word of mouth, the participants themselves, the success of the connections made during the gathering, the recognition and support of the start-ups, the satisfaction and enjoyment of participants and of course social events. Businesspeople like to enjoy themselves too.

The ability to network is often singled out as what sets successful entrepreneurs and directors apart from the herd. Networking, however, is not a skill that can be developed overnight or acquired like a database. It is created over time and requires patience, care and dedication. What's more, it's not just about personal interest. Building a network requires reciprocity, fairness and the ability to inspire confidence.

Those who know Benjumea say she's a born networker, known by all the relevant stakeholders in the area of business creation in Spain, and increasingly in Latin America, given that South Summit has already organized events in Bogota and Mexico City and intends to expand its activities in the region. Benjumea explains that one of the reasons for her success is having cultivated a presence in the right networks, and she recommends other women to grasp the importance to relationships, of being in the right places and participating, of dedicating the time needed to get to know other relevant business players:

> If your colleagues are going for a beer after work, then you go too; your partner can stay at home and look after the children just as well as you can.

Platforms are increasingly the way we do digital and global business, and while most function online, what makes South Summit different is its focus on bringing people together, on face-to-face meetings to identify business opportunities, to find investors, partners and to close deals. I sometimes use the term *animal feedback* to describe how we humans seem to need personal contact to carry out important business deals. For example, while today's millennials tend to meet each other through social networks, after this initial, virtual contact, a personal meeting is needed to cement what until then was merely an intellectual relationship: To close important business or recruit senior directors, it still seems necessary for some kind of physical contact.

Benjumea naturally forms an instantaneous bond with the people she meets. She is expressive and warm, cheerful and outgoing, expansive and approachable. She is totally lacking in the arrogance or distance that often characterizes other people of her experience or level. When discussing her career, her honesty and modesty typically prompt empathy and complicity.

At university, she studied Geography and History, a decision that highlights the importance of the Humanities for businesspeople and that generalist studies provide a solid foundation for developing multiple careers, as opposed to the obsession with specialization. When Benjumea was at university in Spain, after completing a course in the Humanities, most graduates would put themselves forward for a post in the civil service: This was considered the natural option and would provide secure, lifelong employment.

Benjumea failed her first round of entrance exams, as frequently happens, but in her case, it provided her with an opportunity to go into business and pursue something she felt a passion for: "Looking back, I know now that I could never have worked for somebody else."

She describes her professional development as based on "learning by doing," gaining confidence and earning trust along the way. "To begin with," she explains, "I felt unsure, but over time I learned the ropes and proved to myself that I could get things done with hard work, dedication and enthusiasm." She remembers the nerves she felt when she was first interviewed on the radio. The journalist introduced her as Mario instead of María, which helped break the ice. Next came her first television interview, although she is now used to the presence of dozens of cameras at South Summit. But she admits still to a certain thrill at such public events, which she says helps release the adrenalin needed to bring out the best and to keep her on her toes.

At the same time, she seeks to demythologize the challenges she has faced, launching a message of confidence and optimism to all female entrepreneurs: "We're permanently demythologizing things. With hard work and passion it's possible to achieve anything, even if it takes time and effort. We have to overcome stereotypes and clichés, which are myths that disappear like mirages if you commit to overcoming them."

Benjumea initially tried her hand at selling and restoring antiques. Later, toward the end of the 1980s, she set up the highly successful Círculo de Progreso, a company that published guides and provided information about university courses, advising candidates about the best study programs for their interests; this was in the pre-Internet age and when there was little information available. The company morphed into *Infoempleo*, the first major platform to connect university graduates with employers in Spain, creating a new model and changing the recruitment market. This led to *Spain Startup*, a platform connecting stakeholders and start-up founders, and then on to South Summit, a natural evolution, but one that has changed her life and the life of hundreds of entrepreneurs.

The common denominator in these business initiatives is Benjumea's passion and enthusiasm for what she does. She remembers an inspirational anecdote during a presentation by a board member of Johnson & Johnson, who talked in very positive terms about her work, prompting one member of the audience to comment: "Sure, but you've been lucky: everything you've done has excited you," to which the woman replied: "I would say that I've made it exciting."

Benjumea says she has always felt passionate about her business initiatives and the impact they have had on people and society, in areas such as professional development, employment or creating companies. Reflecting her enthusiasm for new ideas, she says she enjoys designing strategies and business plans than the day-to-day administrative work, although she is more than capable of getting down into the weeds of offering a particular service to make sure the client is happy.

Benjumea's family has proved to be an entrepreneurial ecosystem: Her husband, Diego del Alcázar Silvela, is the founder of IE University, while their children, Isabela and Diego, have inherited the same groundbreaking spirit. "What sets my mother apart is her passion and love for what she does and with whom she does it," says her son, adding: "she is not an economist by training, and if you ask her she probably is not at all friendly to numbers or structured business plans, but she compensates this by an amazing drive and fervor at what she does, along with her intuition and experience. My mother has guts, courage, bravery. Obstacles in her path do not stop her."

Benjumea's busy calendar means that the lines between the professional and the personal are often blurred. The family's entrepreneurial ecosystem means that conversations in the home are a mix of the personal, current affairs and business, which is an ongoing enterprise.

When I ask her about her views on inclusion policies, she smiles and says: "I always warn people that I'm politically incorrect." In reality, her views are hardly controversial, and she simply believes in the right to express her opinion based on her experiences. "People often say that men choose other men for senior positions, but my experience is different. If you're available, if they know you, then they'll likely go with you.

> In my case, I was elected Vice-president of the Business Circle based on the years I had spent on as part of any number of groups and associations, of my relationship with a huge number of people. First on SECOT [an organization that works with small businesses in Spain], and then the International Women's Forum, taking part in a range of conferences and committees. A friend encouraged me: 'María, you have to be there, make an effort and go for it' and ten years later I ended up on the board of directors of the representative body for business people in Spain."

At present, as well as running her own company, she is a non-executive director of another business and sits on the boards of several organizations as an advisor.

Benjumea was also the driving force behind *Lidera*, a private-public initiative that has made a big impact in Spain by providing financial support for women attending MBA programs, as well as the right mentoring and coaching to boost their employability and promotion in companies. She is particularly proud when she meets women who were part of Lidera a decade ago and discovers the huge impact it played in transforming their careers. Understanding that the power to change things lays in oneself can make a difference, she says.

As regards the salary gap that the data show exists in many companies, Benjumea's advice to women is typically robust:

> If you really believe your salary is lower than that of men in the same position as you, then talk to the head of human resources and make your case. If you're right, you'll soon see your pay raised. Never hesitate to demand what you see as fair conditions from your employer: they will always come round if you're in the right.

Even Benjumea admits that sometimes even she can run low on enthusiasm and passion: At times like this, her advice is: "Get away, do something else, go somewhere else. A change of activity and a breath of fresh air can sometimes be the best way to see things differently. Like Scarlett O'Hara said, tomorrow is another day; the sun will rise, time puts things in perspective."

Looking back over her career, Benjumea accepts she may no longer be the torrent she once was, but while her career now seems more like a river at its widest, the current flows as fast as ever. She has grown to know herself better, having proved that anything is possible if one applies the right means and sufficient effort, as well as relying on the right people.

> If you want to get ahead quickly, then perhaps it's worth doing things alone, but if you really want to achieve your goals and attain success, then you must find the right team to work with you.

Benjumea says she is still surprised at how much she has achieved and then tempers that by adding that there is still much to be done.

Benjumea's profile is an excellent introduction for the Philosophy we're going to look at, and specifically, two aspects I will focus on. Firstly, the myth that specialization is key to professional success. On occasions, a generalist background, an education rooted in the Humanities, as is the Benjumea's case, is the best foundation for leading people. Secondly, that a passion for what we do is the best way to understand an activity, and that loving somebody else is the best way to know and realize one's strengths and potential, which is fundamental for leading a company. Now, let's continue discussing the advantages of generalist studies versus specialization.

Generalists and Specialists: The Case of Iris Murdoch

Specialization and the creation of university departments throughout the nineteenth century, based on the model proposed by Wilhelm Von Humboldt,[2] have produced significant results, notably a deep academic focus within specific disciplines. Without this specialization, entire scientific areas that have extended our knowledge of the world and helped us find solutions to our problems would not exist.

However, this specialization has its critics, who argue against what they see as the concentration of researchers in overly circumscribed areas, fragmentation or nuclearization of knowledge, along with the silo syndrome, which have led to a disconnect between branches of knowledge, along with compartmentalized research.

In the case of Philosophy, the traditional approach encouraged thinkers to address all manner of subjects and to develop a world view that encapsulated their ideas, but this generalist methodology disappeared as universities created departments specializing in new areas, a process that has led to the highly focused research we see in today's academic journals. We no longer see this generalist approach or efforts to create an overarching theory of the kind associated with the traditional philosophers. In short, the depth that comes from specialist research has come at the cost of abandoning an inter-disciplinary approach.

The professionalization of Philosophy has also prompted two defensive responses from the academic status quo. On the one hand, a critical reaction to writers from outside the university system—typically described as interlopers—along with mistrust toward those academics locked away in their departmental silos.[3] On the other hand, we have seen the exclusion of academics who look not only for feedback from their peers but also public opinion, by sharing their ideas through books and media appearances that provide as wide an audience as possible.

This specialization of philosophical analysis is what Iris Murdoch found when she began teaching at St Anne's College, Oxford University, in 1948, where she contributed actively at conferences and to publications. Reflecting the irony and misogyny widespread in Philosophy at the time, she was dubbed the "Abbess of Oxford"[4] by her overwhelmingly male colleagues. Most historians have placed her within the formidable quartet made up of Philippa Foot, Mary Midgley and Elizabeth Anscombe, all lecturers at Oxford from the generation that lived through World War II as young women and were exposed to the horrors of Nazism and totalitarianism.

At the same time, Murdoch can be seen as an academic outlier, a thinker prepared to swim against the current: In his biography of Murdoch, Peter J. Conradi, quotes Philippa Foot: "We were interested in moral language and she was interested in moral life."[5]

Challenging the metaethical analytical debate of the time, led by R. M. Hare,[6] Murdoch was more interested in raising substantive questions that were relevant to daily life.

Her resistance to academic classification is shown in two characteristics of her work. On the one hand, she mixes writers from different times and schools, transgressing the limits between disciplines and exploring what Stephen Marshall called: "the intermediate zone between Philosophy, secular morality and religious belief."[7] On the other hand, Murdoch combined academic theory with a career as a novelist. Her biographers have discussed which of these two facets were the most important in her life, sometimes calling Murdoch a philosopher who wrote or a novelist who philosophized.

Murdoch wrote 25 novels and was acclaimed by critics and public alike: Her novel *The Sea, the Sea*[8] won the Booker Prize in 1978. Her stories, deeply psychological in the tradition of Balzac and Tolstoy, are populated by characters who explore their inner life, as well as their personal relationships and sexuality, some of whom are undoubtedly based on friends and colleagues. She was a member of the Communist Party in her youth and supported the cause of a united Ireland, the country where she was born. She sought new experiences and her marriage to Oxford don and literary critic John Bayley was an open one. Among her lovers was Nobel laureate Elias Canetti, whose machismo and capacity for seducing women probably provided the inspiration for some of her male characters.

In her later years, Murdoch suffered from Alzheimer's. Her experience was captured in the 2001 film *Iris*, based on her husband's account of her life.

Compassion, Love and Leadership

In *The Sovereignty of the Good*,[9] published in 1970 and arguably her most important work, Murdoch formulated a moral philosophy rooted in Plato, dismissed as outdated by her peers at Oxford, who had embraced naturalism and subjected philosophical arguments to the principles of science and logic. This analytical Philosophy proposed analyzing moral judgments from an objective standpoint, principally focusing on the meaning we give to words and concepts.

In contrast, Murdoch argues that the individual's inner point of view, his or her personal understanding of the world and the people in it, is the benchmark for our moral behavior. In her opinion, science alone cannot explain our beliefs, aspirations, feelings and contradictions. The moral behavior of people cannot be reduced to scientific arguments taken from genetics or psychology, or to use a modern-day analogy, from analyzing big data. Analytical philosophy is not much use either, argues Murdoch, describing it as simply "the picture frame."[10]

To illustrate her thinking and the importance she gave to the individual's inner life, Murdoch uses the analogy of the mother-in-law, who is traditionally associated with displays of animosity toward the daughter-in-law, who is not seen as good enough for the beloved son or sons.

However, Murdoch explains that it is possible to reverse these feelings, to change that negative and critical image. If the mother-in-law instead tries to highlight all her daughter-in-law's positive qualities, making an effort to change her opinion of her perceived defects or even justify them, then it's possible she will be less hostile. Imagine that the mother-in-law strives every day to see some positive aspects of her daughter-in-law, interacting with her like she would her own daughter, forgiving any possible misunderstandings and doing her best to praise her and show affection. Over time, we might reasonably expect the mother-in-law to change her opinion about her daughter-in-law and to end up loving and respecting her.

Murdoch explains that the only way to understand people or things, to know them as fully as possible, is by loving them. The result of this inner exercise is to see things in their best light, from the best angle. "We need a Moral Philosophy within which the concept of love, so rarely mentioned today by philosophers, can once again occupy a central role."[11]

The mother-in-law analogy can be applied directly to managing people in organizations. Given executives' tendency toward action, we quickly classify our work colleagues into friends and enemies. This is part of our animal instinct and allows us to map our working environment, classify people and behave accordingly. But corporate relations can easily turn into a black and white, binary world, with the risk that groups are created whose disputes detract from the pursuit of the common good.

As a rule, we tend to appreciate the people in our own department or those we have personally selected or those who have treated us well. Similarly, it's not unusual to feel hostility toward people who have criticized us or with whom we've argued. Memories remain, and we tend to apply our bias toward our colleagues and coworkers.

In my experience as an educator and manager, personal disagreements are often the result of misunderstandings. For example, the use of short messages via social networks and email can so easily give rise to misinterpretation. Written communication is not as subtle as talking, where facial expressions and tone of voice play a big part. Emoticons can help to sweeten short messages, but my advice is simply to avoid putting into words anything negative or critical, unless you want to upset people.

We should also avoid overreacting when using social networks or email: It is always preferable to resolve distances face to face. Perhaps the best illustration of how an exchange of messages can lead to an uncontrolled spiral is the kind of mutual accusations we find on Twitter. There's an additional disadvantage, best summed in the Latin adage: *verba volant, scripta manent*; words fly, but script remains, in many cases forever.

Another frequent cause of interpersonal misunderstanding is critical comments about us from secondhand sources. Research into the flow of these comments shows how they can be distorted when told by one person to another, even when there is no such intention. I find it's best thing to ignore criticism about me supposedly made by a third party.

A third opportunity for misunderstandings is clustering work colleagues into three groups: friends, enemies and neutrals. Working on the basis of "the enemy of my enemy is my friend," we tend to be aloof, to avoid or even to attack people who are close to those we don't get on with. A variant of this clustering is to reject diversity, distancing ourselves from people who think, look or live differently to us. Research shows the destructive consequences, for individuals as well as collectives, of looking for sameness in others.[12]

It would seem therefore, that this tendency to classify our colleagues in such simple terms is perfectly natural. It's instinctive and a way of mapping our organization so as to know who we can trust. That said, Murdoch's mother-in-law analogy provides the key to overcoming this syndrome, getting to know people better and therefore becoming better leaders. The idea is to put into practice the virtue of compassion, which tends to be defined as "sympathetic consciousness of others," and that allows us to see people from another perspective, based on how we contemplate them in our inner life.

"Compassion is empathy in action," explains US organizational theorist Richard Boyatzis,[13] who has carried out many research projects into how to improve the way groups integrate into organizations. Being compassionate consists of understanding other people as they see themselves, in understanding their aspirations and concerns. To reach this level of understanding, it's necessary not just to increase our knowledge of somebody, which can be done by reading upon them, but by really listening to the way they tell their story about who they are.

"Caring about others is what evokes compassion,"[14] concludes Boyatzis, reflecting the approach taken by Murdoch, who explained from a philosophical perspective that compassion, loving somebody, is the only way to really know them.

Exercising Compassion to Enhance Leadership

Compassion can operate at both the individual and the organizational levels.

In the area of personal development, compassion can be understood as a virtue, which is to say a good habit: Based on repetition of certain practices over time, we can learn to better understand others and therefore increase our capacity for leadership.

There are three specific practices that help cultivate this virtue:

The first is to practice self-compassion. Any number of studies explain how our typical response to professional failure is all too often defensiveness or simply to give up. Neither is positive and makes it difficult to learn from our mistakes, while generating resentment and limiting our professional and personal growth. The best thing to do when faced with failure or mistakes is to be self-compassionate, understand that we all make mistakes, play down the importance of what's happened and cultivate a more sporting approach. This attitude will allow us to keep growing. At the same, and equally important, exercising self-compassion will make us more compassionate of others and therefore allow us to better understand them and to be fairer in our interpersonal relationships. In short, to be better leaders.

Boyatzis offers two exercises that can really help us to better understand the power of compassion. The first involves asking ourselves which people have played a decisive role in our personal and professional development: at which moments in our lives they have helped us, and the advice they offered. In return, we can ask ourselves who we have worried about and helped in a disinterested way.

Boyatzis' research shows that most executives have longstanding memories of those mentors who cared for them and were sincerely interested in their plans for the future, their ambitions and concerns.[15] Also, just over half of executives surveyed remembered colleagues who provided feedback at performance evaluation meetings or when looking at ways to improve working practices. These different responses show the decisive impact that the exercise of compassion can have in orienting the behavior and performance of people we're responsible for.

The second mental exercise for practicing compassion is putting oneself in the other person's position. This type of role-playing is practiced at some business schools to help students embrace diversity. For example, by taking on the role of a member of a minority or somebody from a very different culture to our own or swapping gender so as to better understand the social, cultural and linguistic biases found within the business world.

At the institutional level, we can adopt a range of measures to help create collective awareness of compassion. Senior management obviously has a big role to play in this, as in any initiative to help implant corporate culture. It's also important to see compassion as a value, highlighting its importance in institutional documents and in the company's narrative. More complex, but worth the effort, is including collaboration and mutual assistance as a part of performance evaluation. On the other hand, firms can create coaching and mentorship programs to encourage people to show compassion to others in the organization.

Even after applying Iris Murdoch's recommendations regarding the exercise of compassion toward those we work with, we will still come up against resistance. In these situations, some experts recommend looking for opportunities to work alongside these people so as to get to know them better. And in the final analysis, when none of these things work, it's never a bad idea to ask if perhaps we are the problem.

Genuine compassion is about wanting to know and help others to improve. That said, there is another type of very human compassion, described by the Austrian writer Stefan Zweig in his 1939 book *Beware of Pity*, which can be dangerous: "There are two kinds of pity. One, the weak and sentimental kind, which is really no more than the heart's impatience to be rid as quickly as possible of the painful emotion aroused by the sight of another's unhappiness, that pity which is not compassion, but only an instinctive desire to fortify one's own soul against the sufferings of another; and the other, the only one at counts, the unsentimental but creative kind, which knows what it is about and is determined to hold out, in patience and forbearance, to the very limit of its strength and even beyond."[16]

Takeaways

As in the rest of the book, my fundamental objective is to understand the relationship between the propositions of philosophers and their application to the practice of management. The examples of María Benjumea in the business world and those of Irish Murdoch offer some useful conclusions:

– Both a generalist education and specialization have their pros and cons. A grounding in the Humanities and Liberal Arts cultivates the essential faculties for developing our personality and is an excellent foundation for understanding other people better and for leading cross-cultural teams. Specialization allows us to penetrate more deeply into specific

areas. Ideally, we should combine both approaches as part of our personal education.
- Labels and classifications are frequently used to map reality and to advance our knowledge, associating ideas, concepts and people. That said, there is a very real risk of simplifying things and lapsing into stereotypes, leaving us with nothing more than a superficial understanding of other people.
- The best way to really know somebody else is, in Murdoch's opinion, to love them, trying to see their strengths and positive sides. In the same way, Benjumea believes that professional success in leading a start-up or a business is about having passion for what one is doing, which is not innate, and instead requires personal effort and dedication to the task at hand.
- Compassion, rather than pity, for our colleagues, understanding their aspirations, their family and personal circumstances are the basis of leadership and successful management. At the end of the day, management is about leading people.

Notes

1. The quotes in this section are extracted from an interview between Maria Benjumea and the author, dated August 29, 2019.
2. J. Ostling, *Humboldt and the Modern German University: An Intellectual History*, L. Olsson (trans.) (Lund: Lund University Press, 2018); Ch. 2.
3. R. Craig, College Silos Must Die For Students to Thrive, *Forbes*, April 14, 2017. https://www.forbes.com/sites/ryancraig/2017/04/14/college-silos-must-die-for-students-to-thrive/#20035807222d.
4. P.J. Conradi, Iris Murdoch Obituary: A Witness to Good and Evil, *The Guardian*, 9 February 1999.
5. P. Conradi, *Iris Murdoch, a Life* (New York, NY: W. W. Norton 2001); p. 302.
6. R.M. Hare, *The Language of Morals* (Oxford: Oxford University Press, 1973).
7. M. Antonaccio, Reconsidering Iris Murdoch's Moral Philosophy and Theology, in A. Rowe (ed.), *Iris Murdoch: A Reassessment* (London: Palgrave Macmillan, 2007).
8. I. Murdoch, *The Sea, the Sea* (London: Vintage Classics, Penguin, 2001).

9. I. Murdoch, *The Sovereignty of the Good* (London: Routledge, 2001); references here are made to the Spanish version: *La soberanía del bien*, A. Jaume (trans.) (Madrid: Taurus, 2019); Kindle ed.
10. Ibid., Kindle ed., loc. 807.
11. Ibid., Kindle ed., loc. 1501.
12. S.B. Klein, Sameness and the Self: Philosophical and Psychological Considerations, *Frontiers of Psychology*, January 29, 2014; pp. 5–29.
13. R. Boyatzis and A. McKee, *Resonant Leadership: Renewing Yourself and Connecting with Others Through Mindfulness, Hope, and Compassion* (Cambridge, MA: Harvard Business School Publishing, 2005); Ch. 8.
14. Ibid.
15. Ibid. See also, D. DeSteno, How to Cultivate Gratitude, Compassion, and Pride on Your Team, *Harvard Business Review*, February 20, 2018.
16. S. Zweig, *La impaciencia del corazón*, J. Fontcuberta (trans.) (Barcelona: Acantilado, 2011); Kindle ed., loc. 131.

6

Authenticity: Elizabeth Anscombe/Catherine Moukheibir

A Tale of Three Continents: Catherine Moukheibir[1]

Lebanon, a small, densely populated country hemmed in by the Mediterranean, Israel and Syria, has been a crossroads between Asia, Europe and Africa for millennia. Culturally, religiously and ethnically diverse, its people have shown an extraordinary capacity for integration and inclusion: In recent years, this tiny nation has generously received millions of Syrians fleeing civil war. The Lebanese are famous for their networking abilities, their diplomatic skills and their capacity for management. They are rightly considered the descendants of the Phoenicians, an ancient civilization more interested in trade than conquest.

Like their forebears, the Lebanese continue to migrate around the world, in recent years prompted by invasion and civil war. There are now three times as many Lebanese living abroad than at home, with leading figures in politics, the arts, literature and business recognized around the world, particularly in the Americas. There are also any number of Lebanese, many of them women, occupying top positions in businesses throughout the Middle East. One of the reasons for this presence and visibility in business is that many Lebanese have studied abroad and returned home with an international education and significant cross-cultural skills.

Catherine Moukheibir encapsulates this archetype: cultivated, competent, cosmopolitan and possessing Lebanese, US and British nationality. A Yale MBA, she has accumulated extensive and highly valued experience in the fields of corporate governance and business leadership. She is a renowned expert in biotech companies, sitting on the board of five of them, three of which are publicly traded; Ironwood is a US company on the Nasdaq; Orphazyme, a Danish business on the OMX; and Swiss player GenKyoTex, traded on Euronext. She is also a member of the board of Britain's Kymab and Chairman of the board of France's MedDay Pharmaceuticals, both privately run. Moukheibir owes her success fundamentally to her managerial and financial expertise and also sits on the audit committees of those boards. Her management experience in companies of differing sizes and from different sectors has allowed her to professionalize management at different periods of transition, for example, from start-up to large company.

Her experience in business, as company and bank executive and as a non-executive director on boards, has shaped her holistic thinking about management: "My philosophy of management doesn't distinguish between what I do as a professional manager and my view of what a company is for."

Moukheibir traces her approach to decision-making back to Aristotle: "The practical reasoning theory set out by Aristotle combines factual, value and instrumental reasoning in order to determine what is to be done. For me making decisions this way is the essence of good management." As this book argues, management is about action, about executing decisions with a goal, which also includes the possibility of measuring results. Moukheibir has her own worldview and personal values, but what really counts in life is taking executive decisions and the arguments used to justify them.

> I would characterize what I do as my practice of management, because it is anchored in certain values, and principles. I distinguish between the values of the enterprise and the values of the manager.
>
> My view of the enterprise has implications for how decisions are taken. One of the results I want from any decision-making scenario is that my credibility is maintained.

Within this approach, the basic test for justifying business decisions, particularly those which are difficult and that entail moral dilemmas, is being able to explain them publicly and be able to maintain one's reputation, even if they're controversial. This is something that is taught on MBAs, notably within case studies, and also as part of debates on business ethics. This teaching method encourages open discussion and the use of reasonable argument to convince others of one's case, simulating what happens in reality when a CEO has to justify decisions to stakeholders: "Management is about exercising good judgment to inform decision making, then communicating that decision, clearly, to others, so they implement it."

Decision makers may resort to philosophy, to the Humanities, to find guidelines, arguments and reasons to justify their decisions: "I am a very vocal advocate of studying the Humanities: Literature, Philosophy, the History of Art, as a precursor to business, in the tradition that has been prevalent in the West. In particular, I believe that the study of the Humanities enables the development of innovative thinking and creativity, both of which are hallmarks of excellent management.

> The study of Humanities is one of the best ways to develop judgment capabilities, because the Humanities teach one to be open to contrary arguments about what is to be done and ideally engage in these arguments rather than deflect them. The result is that one acquires the attitude that there is no single right answer to the big questions, such as how people should live their lives or how society should progress, or the role of companies in society, or even what makes a good enterprise."

There is no one-size-fits-all response to business dilemmas, which is why it is particularly important to balance personal criteria with teamwork, along with good governance systems, in companies. Moukheibir stresses the importance of teamwork, particularly in her sector, where creativity and innovation tend to be the result of teamwork rather than individual effort, contradicting the cliché of the lone scientist who comes up with a breakthrough scientific discovery. Awards rewarding the individual, such as the Nobel Prize, underplay the nature of scientific research, which is generally the result of teamwork. "One tenet of my practice of management is team building while retaining personal decision-making authority.

> To illustrate: there is an issue; let people discuss and give their views, which reflect the individuals' knowledge and experience area. I make sense of the discussion. If the answer doesn't fall into place spontaneously, then I solve the problem: how do we get from what people have said to a sound answer, which is not necessarily shared by all. The decision is accepted for reasons of process or substance or both and is settled. I then communicate the decision and that these are now the marching orders. No reopening of the discussion."

Moukheibir is one of those people who looks you firmly in the eye during conversation, creates empathy and is able to express herself through non-verbal communication. She believes a commitment to ethics must be uncompromising and without exception and is one of the most important attributes when leading a company, not just in biotechnology or pharmaceuticals. "Basic examples such as probity, discretion, fairness, equity not equality need to emanate from the top and percolate to the very bottom. The top is responsible at all times for projecting flawless behavior and ethics, which is the glue that holds the organization together."

Consistency between the values, principles and activities of a company are fundamental for Moukheibir, and she considers disagreement to be a "failure of management," which raises one of the most basic questions in philosophy, related to coherence between how we think and how we act.

Moukheibir says she has never suffered from gender discrimination in the business world and that she has benefitted from informal mentoring. At the same time, she recognizes that "men routinely engage in undeniably misogynistic behavior, which women rarely counter by pushing back."

> "As a woman in business, I believe that my university education and early professional career in leading institutions in the United States gave me recognition and credibility, irrespective of my gender. I suspect that it would have been more difficult in Europe, where, in the 1980s when I was a student and young professional, gender still impacted on roles.
>
> More importantly though, I was raised in an environment where I was never treated any differently from the boys and I was educated and promoted in exactly the same way, without any fuss. The result was that I never felt I had to prove anything to anyone other than myself. The cumulation of these two sets of experience shaped my personality to the point that I never even contemplated that being female would be a drawback or, for that matter, an asset to use to get ahead."

There is a shortfall in the number of women studying STEM (Science, Technology, Economics, Medicine) at university, and as a consequence as professionals, but more women are entering Biology and Biotechnology. According to *Catalyst*, the gender and inclusion studies think tank, between 2015 and 2016, the percentage of women studying Biology and Biomedical Sciences was 59% at undergraduate level, 57% at masters and 53% at doctoral level.[2]

However, it's a very different picture regarding the number of women holding senior positions on the advisory boards of biotechnology companies, the bodies that function as bridges between scientific investigation and the business world, the process known as technology or knowledge transfer. Nancy Hopkins and Harvey Lodish, of MIT, have analyzed the phenomenon and shown that despite the number of women studying biology, 95% of board members in biotech company advisory boards are men, and it's the same story everywhere else: "Our experience is that women faculty with greater expertise and stature are often passed over for participating in biotech start-ups in favor of men who are part of the biotech old-boy network (…) We asked the women faculty in Science at MIT if they had been invited to join start-up companies founded by their male colleagues; none had been."[3] They conclude that the departments supervising research transfer and issuing licenses in universities should set their sights on appropriate diversity and inclusion ratios and that the same should apply to venture capital funds investing in the sector.

Moukheibir is one of the few exceptions to this rule, even though she never was formally educated in STEM but was able to bridge this gap by learning the technical aspects on the job over 20 years.

Committed to diversity, in both the biotech and the corporate world generally, Moukheibir believes "diversity is the driver of innovation, because diversity means difference, difference in thinking, problem analysis, solution identification, overall gain from considering otherwise unseen angles. (…)"

> I believe in quotas, directives, and positive discrimination as means to facilitate entry. Once in, the beneficiaries of these policies need to be coached if needed, and then held to the same standards as other employees. This is where a good manager or boss comes in, to act fairly, equitably and strictly with all, and to serve as mentor as needed.

Moukheibir gave me three maxims based on her professional life that might inspire young managers and entrepreneurs as they pursue their careers:

- "God gave you two ears and one mouth, use them in that same proportion." In my experience, this maxim is particularly apt for men to apply when attending meetings with women.
- "Ask for help and clarification unless you understand everything." Using this maxim allows the manager to hold the subordinate accountable for good judgment as to the limitation of their knowledge.
- "Always hire stars," a maxim that confident professionals who are looking to recruit the best team for the job follow.

Beyond biotech, her varied experience in different industries and at all levels of a company has given Moukheibir a holistic vision of business, and she firmly believes that corporate governance has a central role to play in every strategy, in generating sustainable value through better leadership and accountability.

A Thinker Who Stuck to Her Principles: Elizabeth Anscombe

Should philosophers practice what they preach? It could be argued that if philosophy aims to give meaning to our personal lives and shape the values that guide our decisions, then philosophers should be the first to set an example of rationality and integrity.

But then again, why should philosophers be judged differently to other professions? Who hasn't wondered why medics don't live healthier lives? As a boy, I remember doctors smoking in their surgeries and what about lawyers who will go to any length to win a case, including breaking the law, while some architects live in very different homes to those they design for the rest of us. It seems there are many contradictions inherent to certain professions and even to some aspects of life, an ancient phenomenon captured in the Biblical proverb "Physician, heal thyself."

Furthermore, we should bear in mind that the professionalization of philosophy has converted it into an activity largely carried out within the confines of academia, with a clear dividing line between the private and professional spheres. In recent years, this distinction has been further underscored, helped by the anonymity urban societies afford, as well as by management practices. Work is one thing; who we are as individuals is quite another, a dichotomy that might be the result of circumstance, motivation or contradictory principles: "My house is my kingdom" goes the refrain, delimiting the private area where we are free and do not have to account for our actions.

Equally, this seeming contradiction among philosophers might be explained in terms of human frailty: We all aspire to excellence, but we also know that our own limitations, vices or lack of willpower often prevent us from attaining it.

That said, there have been philosophers who embodied the ideals of integrity and consistency between their beliefs and their actions. The archetypal thinker prepared to make the ultimate sacrifice for his beliefs is Socrates, who accepted a death sentence he considered unjust because he believed in the higher principle of obedience to legitimate authority. The Greek thinker spent his final hours surrounded by his disciples speculating

6 *Authenticity*: Elizabeth Anscombe/Catherine Moukheibir

about the immortality of the soul before dutifully downing his cup of hemlock.[4]

Other philosophers have also exposed themselves to danger for refusing to compromise their ideas. Rousseau finally emigrated to Switzerland, while Descartes chose lengthy stays in Sweden to avoid the wrath of the Catholic Church. Plato, Hobbes and Machiavelli fled into exile.[5] But all in all, philosophy has proved to be a less dangerous occupation than politics or even science, although sadly, there are still many countries around the world where thinkers are persecuted for their ideas.

Gertrude Elizabeth Margaret Anscombe, who died in 2001 at the age of 81, provides us with an outstanding example of a modern philosopher whose commitment to her beliefs led her to speak out publicly against what she considered injustice. In 1956, she opposed Oxford University's decision to award an honorary degree to Harry S. Truman[6] (5), arguing that the US president was responsible for the deaths of thousands of innocent civilians after ordering atomic bombs be dropped on Hiroshima and Nagasaki in the closing days of the World War II. Her opposition was not based on her politics, but was instead the conclusion of the philosophical analysis developed in her work: Several of her essays explore the concepts of intentionality and causality with the aim of establishing when we are responsible for our actions, independently of their consequences.[7]

Even more controversial was Anscombe's staunch opposition to the use of birth control, particularly in Africa. Anscombe, who was better known by her initials, G.E.M., had converted to Catholicism in her youth, as had her husband, Peter Geach, a fellow academic, with whom she had seven children. Her opposition to the use of contraceptives reflected her commitment to Vatican doctrine, prompting much criticism from her colleagues, a number of whom successfully demonstrated the conceptual weakness of her arguments in this regard. She was also opposed to abortion rights, another example of what some of her colleagues diplomatically described as her "outspokenness," an unusual quality among British academics at the time.[8]

Anscombe had been a disciple of the great Austrian philosopher Ludwig Wittgenstein at Cambridge in the 1930s and was later named by him as the executioner of his work: In 1953, she translated his *Philosophical Investigations*.[9] Wittgenstein's influence shows through in Anscombe's thinking, for example, the importance he made of examining the use of ordinary language when constructing conceptual propositions. The combination of Wittgenstein's influence and Anscombe's Catholicism has also placed her among the analytical thomists, a philosophical movement that sought an exchange between the ideas of thirteenth-century theologian Thomas

Aquinas and contemporary analytical philosophy. Like Wittgenstein, Anscombe was not trying to create an overarching philosophical theory, but instead sought to address specific questions.

That said, she differed from Wittgenstein, who distrusted people who publicly defended moral choices.[10]

Anscombe acquired an early reputation as a fine speaker after defeating C.S. Lewis, himself a conservative Anglican, at a historic debate held at the Oxford Socratic Club in 1948. Lewis's subsequent decision to give up philosophy and focus on writing is often attributed to his run in with Anscombe. Mary Geach, Anscombe's daughter, later explained the event in terms of the difference between a philosopher and a sage: "The way to show respect for a sage is to accept his teaching, but the way to respect the philosopher is to argue."[11]

Anscombe was certainly possessed of a formidable capacity for concentration and would often give lectures without the use of notes, establishing a style more akin to thinking out loud. Michael Dummett, a colleague during her time at Oxford, summed up her rigor and discipline:

> After *Philosophical Investigations* was published, she presided over a group to discuss it at her house. During that term, she had a baby, and I heard that the labour was extremely difficult. Assuming that the discussion group would be cancelled, I went round the next day with a bottle of wine for a celebration. I found Elizabeth in a dressing-gown and the discussion in full swing; she merely glanced at me, remarking that I was late.[12]

Anscombe continued to write throughout her life, even after retiring from Cambridge University, where she spent the latter years of her career. She suffered from a heart condition as she grew older, but her death in 2001 was most likely brought on by injuries suffered in a car accident.

Speaking Out: When CEOs Have to Stand up for Their Principles

The first aspect of Anscombe's philosophy and life that can be applied to management theory is a public commitment to one's values and principles, a practice demanded of politicians, philosophers and academics, though it may not always be sincere or authentic. But while managers and entrepreneurs may hold opinions about pressing social issues such as inequality, immigration, sustainability or populism, expressing them in public has often resulted in undesired consequences. In the world of business, the more senior one's position, the greater the risk of scrutiny and disagreement with all kinds of stakeholders.[13]

For this reason, people in senior positions, such as CEOs and board members, have tended to be circumspect about what they say in public regarding moral or ethical questions and have been reluctant to join in public debates, preferring instead to focus exclusively on defending the interests of their shareholders and customers, to whom, in the final analysis, they are accountable.

Another reason CEOs might choose to keep their thoughts to themselves is concern over the reaction from the authorities, particularly in state-regulated sectors. In some countries, falling foul of the government can lead to restrictions on business activities, fines and even expropriation.

Nevertheless, business leaders are increasingly finding themselves under pressure to clarify their position on issues their forebears were able to avoid addressing. Accountability and sustainability now mean CEOs must take into account the views of a wider group of stakeholders and indeed society in general, based on the size and impact of the business they represent.

Social responsibility has come to be seen as an integral part of a company's overall strategy[14] and how it communicates with society, giving CEOs a more active role in debates about the pressing issues of the day, which in some cases has contributed to bringing about change: The decision by many companies in the 1980s to boycott South Africa arguably hastened the end of apartheid.

More recently, in Spain, in a move clearly intended to send a warning to the Catalan independence movement, most of the largest companies based in Catalonia moved their headquarters to Madrid and other cities in response to the regional government in Barcelona's illegal declaration of independence in 2017, a decision based on a tantalizing vision that was not supported by the majority of the electorate and other key stakeholders.[15]

In 2017, US President Donald Trump's refusal to condemn white supremacists following violent clashes in Charlottesville prompted criticism from the CEOs of some large US corporations, with a number abandoning a White House business advisory council in protest.[16]

Let me say now that I am not proposing that CEOs and managers should necessarily join in every debate. Any decision to comment on the issues of the day should be made after weighing up the strategic impact and based on arguments that, broadly speaking, reflect the company's outlook and philosophy.

Obviously, there are situations where basic democratic principles are under attack, requiring a robust response from business leaders. This leads us on to Anscombe's proposition that there are principles and moral positions that are absolute and that have primacy over any other considerations.

Consequentialism and Absolutism: The Business Case and the Moral Case

There are three main philosophical theories of morality, the models that guide how we should act. In this section, I'll look at the first two, deontology and consequentialism, which are typically seen as opposing. I'll leave my analysis of the third group, theories of virtue, for the chapter devoted to Philippa Foot.

Deontological theories tie in with classical Greek moral philosophy and state that correct decisions are based on the application of rules and principles to specific situations. Good and bad therefore come down to applying these rules and principles, independently of the consequences. Late eighteenth-century German philosopher Immanuel Kant is perhaps the best-known exponent of this group of theories; he used the example of never lying, even to the murderer at the door who asks the whereabouts of his victim.[17]

The limits of deontological theories to provide a full, satisfactory answer to moral questions, and the supposed inadequacy of Kant's proposition, have persuaded many philosophers to modulate and perfect his arguments or to look for alternatives. Consequentialism, the other major group of moral theories posits that the rightness or wrongness of an action or decision is based on the outcomes and thus should ignore other principles or rules. One modality is utilitarianism, the classical interpretation of which holds that the best decision is the one that is most useful for the greatest number of people.

Anscombe is attributed with inventing the term consequentialism in reference to theories that defend the morality of an action based on its consequences or outcomes.[18] In her opinion, these theories did not provide the best solution in deciding which actions are morally right because they do not take intentionality into account. Anscombe explains that some of the consequences of an action, even when foreseen, can still be unintentional, thus ruling out personal responsibility.

Philosophers with an interest in the economy have overwhelming preferred consequentialist theories, probably because economic models link decisions with their outcomes, which can be measured. Among the best-known proponents of utilitarianism are British nineteenth-century thinkers Jeremy Bentham[19] and John Stewart Mill[20] and more recently Indian economist Amartya Sen.[21]

For the same reasons, it is easy to understand why many business leaders would choose consequentialist theories to decide which actions are right or wrong. Generally speaking, strategic decisions in business are justified by their economic impact and many models used for making decisions are based on forecasts of their likely outcome. Many people emphasize that what counts in business, all things considered, is the bottom line. Obviously, some would challenge this statement, adding that this a truism in need of further explanation.[22]

The consequentialist approach can sometimes also be seen in work that seeks to justify decisions related to corporate social responsibility based on their financial impact, the so-called business case. For example, the argument is that ethical behavior will improve economic performance and increase profits.[23]

As mentioned, Anscombe criticized consequentialist theories from a number of positions. Firstly, because they do not make the proper connection between intention and outcome, secondly, because they do not connect the link and are not conclusive regarding the correlation between cause and outcome, and thirdly, because a positive outcome cannot be explained convincingly: What is the utility of an individual or the aggregate utility of individuals in a society? Any answer to this question is disputable both conceptually and morally.

But Anscombe's fundamental argument focuses on the idea that there are principles and rules that are absolute and applicable to any situation, regardless of the outcome. This position tends to be called moral absolutism, a term that while it has a certain negative connotation, reflects the strength and stringency of moral principles under any circumstance, according to Anscombe. To illustrate this, she uses the example of killing the innocent. "But if someone really thinks, in advance, that it is open to question whether such an action as procuring the judicial execution of the innocent should be quite excluded from consideration – I do not want to argue with him; he shows a corrupt mind."[24]

One example of the difference between deontological and consequentialist theories can be found in the justification of diversity policies that companies are now required to implement. Recent literature on diversity policies has tended to focus on the benefits in terms of innovation, creativity, improved atmosphere in the workplace, reduced staff turnover, access to a broader demographic and to reach more stakeholders. One of the most cited sources backing diversity from this perspective is a 2007 McKinsey report showing that publicly traded businesses with a greater number of female board members showed an 11.4% Return On Investment (ROE), compared to the average in their sector of 10.3%.[25]

However, some analysts have questioned the science behind these conclusions, suggesting that the cause and effect between adopting diversity policies and ROE have not been fully established. For example, perhaps the more direct causal relationship is that between a company's size, its growth rate and its ROE. As things stand, a greater number of women hold senior positions in middle-sized companies than they do in large corporations: We might, therefore, conclude that the relationship between the ROE in medium-sized companies and greater gender diversity is circumstantial rather than causal.[26]

I make these points because it is important to understand the motives for implementing diversity policies in a company. In the majority of cases, there are two main arguments for doing so:

The business case, which adopts a consequentialist approach, explains that diversity policies are beneficial for companies both economically and for other, less tangible reasons. This is a supposedly scientific focus, based on empirical evidence of the impact of diversity on businesses' financial results.

The moral case, which entails a deontological conception, argues that the board should encourage diversity in their companies as a way of promoting equality in business and the wider world. In other words, these kinds of policies are the result of moral and ethical decisions, independent of the economic impact on the company, although obviously the hope is that it will be positive.

The majority of CEOs and CLOs I know subscribe to both the moral and the business case to validate their diversity initiatives. They look for evidence of the cost-effectiveness of such measures and need to show their shareholders that diversity has a direct influence on the organization's activities. If they were unable to prove this correlation between diversity and economic results, it would be harder for them to impose diversity policies.

But as said, the hard evidence of a relationship between implementing diversity policies and a bottom line in the black is not easy to find and the research that supports it tends to be anecdotal and circumstantial.

Takeaways

To conclude with Anscombe, the key question here is whether in business it is worth applying certain absolute principles or rules, regardless of their outcome. Along with diversity, this area of decision-making might also include, among others, respect for human rights, animal welfare, protecting the environment and combatting global warming.

– We should remember that in business, pragmatism and compromise are very much the order of the day. Managers are constantly caught between the need to generate immediate and positive results, although that may create secondary, undesired, effects that are unavoidable.
– The important thing, as I have reiterated throughout this book, is to be able to justify these difficult decisions through reasonable arguments, perhaps based on consequentialist or deontological premises directed at convincing a company's stakeholders. As Warren Buffet argued, the acid test of a decision's morality is being able to publish it on the front page of a newspaper the next day.[27]

Notes

1. This section's quotes are extracted from a written interview with Catherine Moukheibir, July 2019.
2. Catalyst, *Women in Science, Technology, Engineering and Mathematics (STEM): Quick Take*, June 14, 2019.
3. N. Hopkins and H. Lodish, *Biotech Has a Woman Problem*, ASCB, Career Navigator Careers, March 21, 2018. https://www.ascb.org/careers/biotech-woman-problem/.
4. Plato, *Phaedo* (Oxford: Oxford University Press, 2009).
5. A classic study the lives and the ideas of philosophers through the ages is F. Copleston's monumental work: *History of Philosophy*, in several volumes (Mahwah, NJ: Paulist Press, 1950).
6. R. Teichman, *The Philosophy of Elizabeth Anscombe* (Oxford and New York: Oxford University Press, 2008); p. 4.

7. G.E.M. Anscombe, *Ethics, Religion and Politics: Collected Philosophical Papers of G. E. M. Anscombe* (Oxford: Blackwell, and Minneapolis: University of Minnesota Press, 1981); p. iii. And *Intention* (Cambridge, MA: Harvard University Press, 2000).
8. G.E.M. Anscombe, *La filosofía analítica y la espiritualidad del hombre: Lecciones en la Universidad de Navarra*, J.M. Torralba and J. Nubiola (eds.) (Pamplona: Eunsa, 2005).
9. L. Wittgenstein, *Philosophical Investigations*, G.E.M. Anscombe (trans.) (Oxford: Basil Blackwell, 2008).
10. R. Teichman, *The Philosophy of Elizabeth Anscombe*, op. cit., p. 4.
11. G.E.M. Anscombe, *Human Life, Action and Ethics*, M. Geach and L. Gormally (eds.) (St. Andrew's Studies in Philosophy and Public Affairs) (Exeter: Imprint Academic, 2005); Introduction, p. xxi.
12. *The Tablet*, January 13, 2001, cit. in R. Teichmann, *The Philosophy of Elizabeth Anscombe*, op. cit., p. 6.
13. D. Gelles, C.E.O. Activism Has Become The New Normal, *The New York Times*, July, 25, 2018, where the author mentions a survey by Weber Shandwick that reveals that: (1) People are increasingly aware of C.E.O. activism. More than a third view it favorably and (2) less than 40% of respondents believe C.E.O.s "have a responsibility" to speak out. About two-thirds of Republicans said C.E.O.s should "stick to business." https://www.nytimes.com/2018/07/25/business/dealbook/ceo-activism-study.html.
14. Vid. the very interesting collection of studies that focuses on the contribution of entrepreneurs and family businesses to CSR: F. Farache, G. Grigore, A. Stancu, and D. McQueen (eds.), *Responsible People: The Role of the Individual in CSR, Entrepreneurship and Management Education* (Palgrave Studies in Governance, Leadership and Responsibility) (London: Palgrave Macmillan, 2019).
15. M. Stothart, Catalan Business Exodus Signals Deep Corporate Concern. Fears over 'Loss of Competitiveness' If Region Is Left Outside the EU and Subject to Tariff, *Financial Times*, October 15, 2017. https://www.ft.com/content/e91df296-b00d-11e7-beba-5521c713abf4.
16. Michael D. Shear and Maggie Haberman, Trump Defends Initial Remarks on Charlottesville; Again Blames 'Both Sides', *The New York Times*, August 15, 2017. https://www.nytimes.com/2017/08/15/us/politics/trump-press-conference-charlottesville.html.
17. I. Kant, develops his *Theory of Right* in *The Metaphysics of Morals*, M. Gregor (trans.), R.J. Sullivan (introd.) (Cambridge: Cambridge University Press, 1996).
18. G.E.M. Anscombe, *Modern Moral Philosophy*, 33 Philosophy, January 1958, p. 124.

19. J. Bentham, *The Collected Works of Jeremy Bentham: An Introduction to the Principles of Morals and Legislation*, J.H. Burns and H.L.A. Hart (eds.) (Oxford: Clarendon Press, 1982).
20. J.S. Mill, *Utilitarianism* (London: Broadview Press, 2000).
21. A. Sen, *Utilitarianism and Beyond* (Cambridge: Cambridge University Press, 1982).
22. M. Sandel, *What Money Can't Buy: The Moral Limits of Markets* (New York, NY: Farrar, Straus and Giroux, 2012).
23. Vid. for example, S. Iniguez de Onzono, *Cosmopolitan Managers: Executive Education That Works* (London: Palgrave Macmillan, 2016); Ch. 7.2.
24. G.E.M. Anscombe, *Modern Moral Philosophy*, op. cit., 40.
25. G. Desvaux, S. Devillard-Hoellinger, and P. Baumgarten, *Women Matter: Gender Diversity, a Corporate Performance Driver* (New York: McKinsey & Company, 2007).
26. UK Government, Department for Business Innovation & Skills, *The Business Case for Equality and Diversity: Survey of the Academic Literature*, BIS Occasional Paper No. 4, January 2013. http://www.raeng.org.uk/publications/other/the-business-case-for-equality-and-diversity.
27. Taken from Berkshire Hathaway Inc., *Code of Business Conduct and Ethics*, quoted in S. Iniguez de Onzono *The Learning Curve: How Business Schools Are Re-inventing Education* (London: Palgrave Macmillan, 2011); p. 27.

7

Humanity: Martha Nussbaum/Olga Urbani

A Company Rooted in the Humanities: Urbani Tartufi[1]

"Italy's green heart" is the oft-used phrase to describe Umbria, the sinuous region, half mountain, half hillside, to the northeast of Rome. The Apennines, Italy's backbone, runs north–south through Umbria, and from which flow the many tributaries of the River Tiber. Among them, to the south, is the Nera, which gives its name to one of Italy's most productive valleys, the Valnerina, which produces 45% of the country's truffles.

The truffle is one of nature's rarities, a fungus that grows within the roots of a tree, creating a symbiotic relationship known as mycorrhiza: The truffle provides its host with minerals and water, receiving in turn carbohydrates and vitamins. Because truffles are found at least 20 centimeters under the soil, they can only be located using specially trained dogs or pigs.

Demand for these culinary diamonds has created a fast-growing international market. Originally, Italy, France and Spain were the only producers, but new biotechnological techniques have allowed the United States, Chile and Argentina to set themselves up as competitors. Furthermore, Italian cuisine, popular around the world, and which uses truffles, has boosted demand. At the same time, gastronomy and nutrition are now rightly considered part of our collective cultural heritage, worthy of the same recognition as other expressions of human development and civilization and part of the Humanities, along with art, literature and music.

The family-run Italian companies I have known, both large and small, and regardless of their sector, have always placed great emphasis on culture, tradition and the arts. It's as though the Humanities were part of every Italian's DNA. Just about every village, town and city radiates history, art and music.

The Valnerina valley is home to a business founded by the Urbani family 170 years ago, Urbani Tartufi, the world's leading producer of truffles, and which distributes 70% of global truffle output, with a growing presence in high-end and specialist food stores in Europe, Asia and the Americas. Revered by food lovers everywhere and the subject of many a glossy magazine profile, Urbani is constantly researching and developing the science of truffles.

"Truffles are a miracle," explains Olga Urbani, the company's CEO and a member of the sixth generation of the family, and who has led the internationalization of the business over the last two decades. With the help of her two sons, Luca and Francesco, she is now adapting the company to the new digital environment. Olga defines the company's culture simply:

> My values can be summarized in one sentence: we are one big family dedicated to producing truffles. For me, my company and my 300 employees are my family. Scheggino, where the company is based, is a very small village where most people work for the company. There are no other jobs around. So it's like a family, sometimes I have to be strict, sometimes I have to be like a mother and other times like a sister.

Olga explains that she learned a great deal from her father and her uncle in a highly secretive business that handed down closely guarded know-how through the generations. She worked with them for several years, gradually assuming more responsibilities. When she began presiding over meetings in a sector traditionally dominated by men, her workers would ask, "when is Signor Urbani arriving?", referring to her father. "Initially, it was discouraging, but over time I realized I had to replace my father and I gradually won them over. For me, the issue was never about being a woman; I may have had to deal with my father as a woman sometimes, but I had no problems dealing with the world as a woman. The only thing that matters in business is professionality, what we call in Italian *competenza* (competency). This is what gives you credibility and earns the respect of the people around you."

Olga confesses that while she was deeply affected by the death of her father, her responsibilities meant that she could not be seen to falter in any way. In situations like this, people who have been brought up in the expectation of leadership find an inner resilience that enables them to respond to the problems they face. Biology plays a role here, as well, in that the brain increases adrenalin production.

> I had very little time, because the business is so demanding and every five minutes you have to answer somebody's question, so sometimes you have no choice and no time. You're at the center, you must do what's needed and you have no choice. I cried at night while during the day I was working and running the company… but always thinking of my father and my family.

Having taken over the role of CEO, Olga now found herself leading the company's reconversion as part of a strategy to make it leaner and more competitive. In a family business with a strong paternalist tradition, undertaking reforms to cut costs was a challenge, but Olga explains that people understand change when it is explained in a realistic and reasonable manner:

> My values are based on the ideal of humanity, of nurturing good relationships with my employees, sometimes explaining things directly, but always politely, and letting them understand what we're going to do and why, explaining why we have taken this or that decision and making people part of my vision.

In the event, Olga lost just two of her forty managers, adding that leaving was the right thing for them to do. She is a firm believer in values such as loyalty, unity and commitment, insisting that these are central to any family business.

The humanist spirit so characteristic of Italy is very much a part of Olga Urbani's vision. Reflecting on this, she has created a visitors' center at the company's HQ that explains both the science and the business behind truffle production, as well as the history of Urbani Tartufi. The idea for the initiative came after she put her father's papers in order as she prepared for her role as CEO.

Delving into the family archives she uncovered all manner of documentation and letters dating back several generations that provided a detailed account of how the company had pioneered the production of truffles. Successive leaders have developed an institution with a profoundly humanist background and a sense of history that has not only strengthened the traditions and customs of the company it is rooted in, but also established itself as a major international business.

Olga's story reflects her humanist vocation. She studied law at Perugia University and obtained her doctorate in jurisprudence. She says her legal training has allowed her to better understand the advice of lawyers when taking major decisions. She finished her education with a Master's from Columbia University, where she says her contact with other business leaders not only helped with networking, but opened her eyes to new ideas. Olga's hasn't been a lineal education focused solely on Management, but instead one that has included the Humanities, which, as we will see later, is characteristic of so many outstanding CEOs. Indeed, the Humanities are the cement that bonds different sciences and areas of knowledge and that managers who cultivate them have a better understanding of the world and the people in it.

Olga says that empathy is one of the key virtues leaders should possess, and that when interviewing men and women for senior posts in the company, she is always looking for their ability to understand other people. She confesses that she often forms an opinion quickly, based on non-verbal language such as how people smile, and that she's rarely wrong. Interestingly, I have seen this intriguing skill in other senior executives with a background in the Humanities. Cultivated people with a genuine love of knowledge—not pedants—also tend to be the most empathetic.

The Measuring Malaise and Its Critics: Martha Nussbaum

The Humanities have been at the core of academic studies since the creation of the first universities in the thirteenth century, when the classics formed part of the "cuadrivium" of music, arithmetic, geometry and astronomy, which would become the basis for the liberal arts education found in many US colleges over the last two centuries.

In recent years, many governments around the world have carried out educational reforms, from K-12 to university level, as well as through continuous education policies. The basic mantra guiding these reforms has been to link learning to measurable results in order to assess whether curricula are improving access to higher education, providing students with the jobs they want, or the skills the labor market requires. We might call this phenomenon *measurism*, the evaluation of the success of an educational program based on supposedly quantifiable and comparable learning outcomes.

One of the main factors driving *measurism* is international education rankings such as the OECD's Pisa,[2] which assess the performance of high school students in various areas, particularly in quantitative subjects such as mathematics. There are also a number of well-known rankings of universities, most of which have been criticized for their methodological deficiencies, but that have anyway proved popular with students looking to attend a renowned institution. We have seen the emergence of a whole area of business based on *measurism*, with companies such as Pearson defining "efficacy" as one of its core values.[3] There has also been an explosion of ed-tech start-ups, squaring what some see as a not entirely virtuous circle.[4]

Martha Nussbaum is among the best-known critics of *measurism*. Currently, the Ernst Freund Distinguished Service Professor of Law and Ethics at the University of Chicago, where she has a dual affiliation with the School of Law and the Department of Philosophy, an interdisciplinary role, which in my opinion, is a very creative and promising avenue for research and the advancement of knowledge, though unusual and not sufficiently fostered at universities.

Nussbaum has researched classical philosophy, applied ethics, political philosophy and jurisprudence, linking the study of classics with social policy. Her most recent book, *The Monarchy of Fear*,[5] published in 2016, warns of the dangers to our societies from hate speech, which is increasingly being propagated at the highest levels as well as through social networks. She proposes as an alternative, constructive, public discourse of the kind used by influential leaders of change like Martin Luther King Jr., Mahatma Gandhi or Nelson Mandela, who maintained their confidence in democratic institutions, the rule of law and the wisdom of ordinary people, as Aeschylus did in Ancient Greece—here again, Nussbaum links antiquity with modernity.

In the 1980s, working with Nobel Economics Laureate Amartya Sen, Nussbaum developed the "Capabilities Approach," an alternative to welfare economics based on the argument that government policies in most western democracies still ignore our most basic human needs for dignity and self-respect.[6] Instead, we need to take an approach to economic development that will enable people everywhere to live full and creative lives. In a fully democratic society, these kinds of capabilities are what allow us to talk about a good life.

Nussbaum has also contributed to the discussion on the need to recognize freedom of sexual orientation and LGBTQI rights. In *From Disgust to Humanity: Sexual Orientation and Constitutional Law*,[7] written in 2010, she revisits the debates of the 1950s and 1960s in the UK over the legalization of homosexuality, when British judge Lord Devlin opposed decriminalization, as proposed by the Wolfenden Report. It is worth remembering that as late as 1959, English courts could categorize sodomy as an act of treason, in that homosexuals were believed to corrupt the collective morality, considered a common good.[8]

Nussbaum criticizes Devlin for his position that it was possible to pass laws prohibiting any act or conduct that would cause "disgust" among the population, even between consenting adults. Nussbaum explains that "disgust" has been the alibi for racist, sexist and anti-Semitic laws down the centuries and has been at the center of hate campaigns toward minorities that enflame public opinion through populist discourse. Nussbaum proposes, in the liberal tradition, that the only limits on the freedom of an adult are that formulated by J.S. Mill in *On Liberty*: "That principle is, that the sole end for which mankind are warranted, individually or collectively, in interfering with the liberty of action of any of their number, is self-protection. That the only purpose for which power can be rightfully exercised over any member of a civilized community, against his will, is to prevent harm to others. His own good, either physical or moral, is not a sufficient warrant."[9]

This principle has been the key to liberalism's defense of human rights and freedoms, confronting the potential oppression of minorities and even impeding practices of legal paternalism that, although well intentioned, restrict our freedom to act against our own well-being, for example, bans on smoking, consuming drugs or alcohol or the requirement to wear seat belts. Furthermore, as some contemporary philosophers have explained, not all bans and responsibilities are the work of the so-called nanny state, but are required for more practical reasons. The use of seat belts, for example, is to avoid the financial cost to our public health service of treating the injuries produced by traffic accidents.[10]

As mentioned earlier, Nussbaum has also fought against the reductionism derived from excessive *measurism* in education. She criticizes educational reforms that only emphasize the importance of STEM, given their supposed relationship with labor market demands, as short term. These initiatives focus mainly on preparing students for executing some specific jobs but neglect the development of an integral personality. I would argue that most teachers would agree that the results of education are only fully tangible in the long term.

That said, we use procedures to measure certain indicators of teaching quality—for example, classroom satisfaction surveys and assessments of teaching methodology. These are sometimes referred to as "happy sheets" because what they really measure is the immediate perception of students following a class. In my experience, feedback from students years later about how an idea or piece of advice mentioned in class is much more satisfying. In addition, there is a growing range of systems to evaluate professional progression over time or assessing the acquisition of knowledge and the development of skills.

Education is a continuous, lifelong activity, and in my opinion, measuring the results of a particular learning initiative is similar to taking a photograph: It provides no more than a snapshot of our personality. The human mind is complex and we know, from experience, that we associate ideas and knowledge with events over time and that our intuition, while established in the early years of education, becomes more sophisticated as it is nurtured with new experiences.

Why Studying the Humanities Makes More Sense Than Ever

As mentioned, the revisionist context of curricula encouraged by many governments has prioritized STEM subjects. The belief is that in a world increasingly dominated by digital technology, the Humanities now play a secondary role. Nussbaum argues that exorcising the Humanities from curricula impinges on achieving other relevant educational goals such as the practice of civic virtues, developing the creative imagination and critical thinking. She believes, in line with classical thinking from Aristotle to Cicero, that the Humanities play a fundamental role in the development of global citizens, as well as in the development of our democracies.[11]

Among the arguments I often use when defending the study of the Humanities is a comparison between the US and European university systems. The education system in continental Europe is largely based on the abovementioned ideas of the German nineteenth-century academic Wilhelm Von Humboldt, whereby university students attend specialized programs from the first year onward with the sole aim of achieving the best preparation for jobs after graduation. For example, mining engineers study subjects like geology from the beginning, which correspond to their future profession, rather than spending time on unrelated matters. The same applies to doctors, architects, lawyers, etc. At the same time, this specialization is reflected in the structure of university departments, which encourage specialized research.

As was Von Humboldt's intention, specialist research has produced a huge leap in science over the last century, matched by exponential growth in academic publications. In the field of degree programs, it has created professionals with highly focused training, ready to join the labor market as long as their knowledge and skills adjust periodically to the changing demands of companies and institutions. If programs do not change, which unfortunately happens due to resistance to change in some university departments and professional associations, curricula are rendered obsolete.

In contrast, many US universities and colleges offer a generalist degree program, typically focused on the Humanities and the Liberal Arts, with specialization taking place at Master's or equivalent level.

Having described the two university systems in this general way, I usually ask my audience the following question: Which of the two produces more entrepreneurs? The unanimous response is usually the US system. I won't go into the details of how entrepreneurship works in both continents, and while my approach may lack scientific rigor, it certainly reflects the entrepreneurial spirit instilled in so many US graduates. My point is that the study of the Humanities, offered by many US colleges, far from prejudicing innovation and entrepreneurship, in fact, favors it.

This is also the conclusion of venture capitalist Scott Hartley, who questions the division of university programs into the arts and the sciences in his 2017 book, *The Fuzzy and the Techie: Why the Liberal Arts Will Rule the Digital World*.[12] At Stanford University, fuzzies is the term used to describe students of the social sciences and Humanities; techies are those enrolled in engineering and hard sciences. Hartley argues convincingly that despite the best efforts of universities to maintain this traditional separation, there are any number of technological entrepreneurs with a background in Humanities.

The traditional separation between the Humanities—the fuzzies—and the sciences—the techies—is based on the common belief that people are predisposed to one discipline or another. This approach guides education from the earliest years and of course determines students' career opportunities after graduation, as well as their salaries, promotion and mobility opportunities, among others. Moreover, it consecrates professional paths that are difficult to cross or change. There is little room for outliers who may work on the verge of professions or for those wanting to switch careers over their lives.

Instead, let's imagine that instead of prolonging this divisive model, schools and universities provided a solid grounding in the natural sciences and the Humanities with the goal of encouraging a more rounded personality in our students. Wouldn't this be so much more positive?

Hartley cites the following cases in support of this integrative approach: Stewart Butterfield, founder of communications platform Slack, studied Philosophy at the University of Victoria and the University of Cambridge;

LinkedIn founder Reid Hoffman took a Master's in Philosophy at the University of Oxford. Peter Thiel, co-founder of Paypal, studied Philosophy and Law. Ben Silbermann, founder of Pinterest, studied political science at Yale. Airbnb founders Joe Gebbia and Brian Chesky graduated in Fine Arts at the Rhode Island School of Design. Steve Loughlin, founder of RelateIQ, studied Public Policy. Parker Harris, co-founder of Salesforce, studied English Literature at Middlebury College. Carly Fiorina, former CEO of Hewlett-Packard, majored in Medieval History and Philosophy, while YouTube CEO Susan Wojcicki studied History and Literature at Harvard and Mark Zuckerberg, founder of Facebook, studied Liberal Arts at the Phillips Exeter Academy before entering Harvard.[13]

Lest we forget, Steve Jobs, who attended liberal arts institution Reed College, said "technology alone is not enough — it's technology married with liberal arts, married with the Humanities, that yields us the result that make our heart sing."[14]

On this same line, Harvard economist David Deming's research shows how soft social skills regularly lead to business teams performing more efficiently. Deming's work highlights the value of soft skills in the labor market: "the fastest growing cognitive occupations – managers, teachers, nurses and therapists, physicians, lawyers, even economists – all require significant interpersonal interaction…"[15]

In short, perhaps we can now leave aside discussion questioning the value of the Humanities in business education. In the first place, as we know, because many of the most important things we learn are only useful in the long term and guide the formation of our personality, our worldview, our beliefs and principles, the mental structure that allows us to order and associate the rest of the knowledge we acquire throughout life.

Secondly, because the education provided by the Humanities is not of a technical or applied nature; it doesn't teach us a specific skill, such as handling a machine or driving a vehicle. Instead, it helps us to develop more abstract capacities related to human development, and as Nussbaum argues so forcefully, the Humanities underpin democratic societies. Therefore, discussion of the "usefulness" of the Humanities is a contradiction in terms, at least if we're talking about how to measure the learning of a specific skill or knowledge directly applicable to a task.

A few years ago I discussed the key role of the Humanities during the French presidential election campaign, prompted by Nicolas Sarkozy's comment that only "a sadist or an imbecile – I leave the choice to you – would have put *The Princess of Cleves* on the syllabus used to test candidates in a public service entrance exam," referring to the seventeenth-century novel.[16]

Sarkozy's comments provoked a barrage of criticism, but perhaps we should also ask why civil servants shouldn't have to answer similar questions to non-nationals who wish to acquire French nationality.

In addition, as I have pointed out, reading literature develops a series of skills that are more useful in the long term for civil servants in their daily contact with the public, rather than merely being taught technical procedures that will soon be carried out by machines or AI. Sarkozy's comment was merely populist bombast, all too common during political campaigns. He was attempting to associate general knowledge with the education of the elites, who may know more about literature because they have attended better schools. There may be some empirical basis to his comments, but they were also perverse, because good politicians should seek to raise educational standards, not lower them.

Management Has Been Ascribed to the Social Sciences…

In terms of its methodology, basic assumptions and scope of knowledge, the science of Management is conventionally included among the social sciences. Businesses are seen, after all, as social entities; they are considered legal personae with an identity and a sense of purposes as unique as that of the individuals who contribute to the whole. This is reflected, for example, in the frequent reference to Management concepts like business culture, understood as the spirit and values consistent with a company's strategy reflected in the behavior of its workers. Or organizational knowledge, related to companies considered as subjects. This mystification is also reflected in institutional theory, embraced by many academics as a conventional starting point to develop their subsequent research on other business phenomena. William Richard Scott explains that "institutions are social structures that have attained a high degree of resilience. [They] are composed of cultural-cognitive, normative, and regulative elements that, together with associated activities and resources, provide stability and meaning to social life. Institutions are transmitted by various types of carriers, including symbolic systems, relational systems, routines, and artifacts. Institutions operate at different levels of jurisdiction, from the world system to localized interpersonal relationships. Institutions by definition connote stability but are subject to change processes, both incremental and discontinuous."[17]

Faced with this configuration of the company as an existing, scientifically observable phenomenon, management guru Sumantra Ghoshal explained in a posthumously published article that "Our theories and ideas have done much to strengthen the management practices that we are all now so loudly condemning."[18] Ghoshal pointed out how the research carried out in many business schools has been aligned with the methodology of the social sciences. This was particularly the case after the recommendations of reports by the Ford and Carnegie foundations in the 1960s, which recommended that business research follows the scientific rigor of sociology or economics. However, as Ghoshal explained, the social sciences suffer from a certain inferiority complex, a "physics envy," with respect to the true sciences because its assumptions, its models and its conclusions lack the definitive character of natural laws.

In sciences such as physics or chemistry, the causal paradigm predominates, while in social sciences the prevailing model is functional, an attempt to explain how individuals behave. Even so, reducing a person's behavior to functional paradigms risks being reductionist, since reality is much more complex. As Ghoshal explains: [no scientific theory]… "*explains the phenomenon of organized complexity*… [of companies] possibly because companies are not empirically observable natural phenomena like volcanoes or animals, or follow any predeterminable pattern."[19]

The result of reducing management as a subject to the level of scientism has been to reduce humans to little more than *homo economicus*, whereby human behavior is simply about satisfying our most basic instincts, says Ghoshal. In parallel, the Chicago School's liberalism insists that companies exist solely to maximize shareholders' return on their investment. As a result, companies have been shaped by institutional theory, with corporate governance based on the need for independent board members, separation of the CEO and the chairman's functions, as well as providing directors with stock options so they share the same interests with the shareholders—all to avoid the risks of applying agency theory.

Ghoshal argues that this leads to an amoral theory of business and questionable behavior. "Unlike theories in the physical sciences, theories in the social sciences tend to be self-fulfilling."[20] In other words, pointing to Enron and Tyco as examples, a vicious circle in which theory and practice feed off each other.

The solution is to understand that there is always an ideology or an intention behind all management theory: "Social scientists carry an even greater social and moral responsibility than those who work in the physical sciences because, if they hide ideology within the pretense of science, they can cause much more harm."[21] In conclusion, Ghoshal calls for better social excellence objectives that reflect the interests of all stakeholders.

...And Management Belongs to the Humanities

Recently, I have begun using conferences as a platform from which to appeal to colleagues in the business school world to move the academic discipline of Management, or at least a good part of it, from the social sciences to the Humanities. In line with other academics, I believe that business practices are best acquired from similar perspectives to those adopted by researchers in disciplines such as history, literature or art. The reasoning used to develop persuasive arguments in the area of strategic management has more to do with the speculative methods than science: The "golden rules" of management are not immutable.

Decision making by senior management is usually underpinned by empirical and quantitative studies. But the hypotheses that underlie much of that reasoning are questionable. It is often said that the environment in which companies operate is not paradigmatic, as, say, with meteorology, where weather conditions can be foreseen for tomorrow considering the available information—although some would question this as well. The business environment is strategic, conditions are constantly changing, and the variation of some circumstance can change forecasts and plans. For example, the emergence of a disruptive company such as Airbnb in the hospitality sector has forced hotels to rethink their business models. We have seen a similar process with new technologies or globalization, which have changed the rules of entire sectors.

It might be countered that it's possible to introduce every circumstance, variation and possibility in a study program that allowed simulations of possible future scenarios so as to focus more accurately on decisions. This is true, and in fact, there are simulations that allow for this kind of evaluation of alternatives and scenarios, and that are used in MBA programs to illustrate the complex nature of strategic reasoning. There are algorithms that simplify all relevant data for a case and then point to the optimal decision. To which I usually ask: Who would you pay more attention to when investing your money, an algorithm or Warren Buffet?

The point is that strategic reasoning is not just complex, and therefore resolvable through sophisticated algorithms; there is an intuitive dimension to it, of association of variables, of thinking outside the box and even without a box. This aspect of strategic business thinking has led academics such as Henry Mintzberg to argue that good management is more an art than a science and is practically impossible to teach through traditional educational systems, and perhaps only by osmosis as a result of contact with other experienced managers.[22]

The good news is that a growing number of philosophers are turning their attention to business and will hopefully facilitate an approach to management from an alternative perspective. Until now, most philosophers interested in the economy have tended to be on the left, which is why companies and business leaders have viewed them with suspicion. Meanwhile, philosophers who have studied organizations have typically been more interested in analyzing the state and government as the major institutions taking collective decisions in society, rather than looking at private organizations and businesses, whose impact has grown over the last century.

Fortunately, the progressive weight of businesses, entrepreneurs and freelancers on the economy has attracted a good number of thinkers to the analysis of business. Most business schools today teach business ethics, while new disciplines such as company philosophy have emerged at the same time as the number of academic and professional publications dedicated to these issues has increased, while more universities are studying in ways that connect philosophy and the business world.

I agree with Nussbaum: We need to create global citizens, cosmopolitan managers and entrepreneurs whose decisions are based on cutting-edge knowledge; men and women who are committed and aware of the social significance of their decisions and the impact on the business environment and who believe in sustainability; they must be cultivated, with a solid grounding in the history, art, literature and culture of different societies, allowing them to lead diverse teams. The Humanities are the cement that holds all knowledge together, and studying them over the course of our lives may be the best way to become and remain a cosmopolitan manager. As CNN's Fareed Zakaria wrote in his 2015 book *In Defense of a Liberal Education*: "creativity, problem solving, decision making, persuasive arguing and Management" are the skills the liberal arts teach us.[23]

Takeaways

Martha Nussbaum's work can provide managers and directors with tremendous insight into how businesses and all organizations work.

- Nussbaum establishes a relationship between tradition and modernity, applying the wisdom of classical thinkers to the reality of the present, illustrating how the major questions we face, regardless of the circumstances, reappear again and again throughout history and are often linked by common threads. It's the same with the work environment. Senior managers who understand the lessons of history, who understand how ideas are born and evolve, who cultivate classical thinking, are able to give greater meaning to their work, placing it within centennial traditions. A sense of history and respect for tradition are perfectly compatible and can help drive innovation, creativity and a forward-looking approach, as so many successful entrepreneurs have shown.

- Measuring results is essential in business, as is setting learning objectives as part of any educational initiative. Nevertheless, an important part of learning only manifests itself over time, sometimes after many years. Furthermore, measuring how our personality has changed is, at least for the time being, pretty much impossible. Tradition and the experience of experts show that studying the Humanities provides many benefits for the development of the personality.
- Trying to measure the "value" of the Humanities misses the point. The objective of the Humanities is to develop cosmopolitan citizens, not to learn a specific skill or technique. Furthermore, the Humanities provide us with the intellectual resources we need to better understand our fellow human beings, strengthening at the same time our capacity for leadership. A significant number of CEOs have studied the Humanities.
- As an academic discipline, Management has traditionally been associated with the social sciences. But I believe that research, teaching and the development of Management skills would all benefit from the additional association of Management with the Humanities.

Notes

1. The quotes in this section are extracted from an interview between Olga Urbani and the author on August 12, 2019.
2. Updates on OECD's Pisa survey may be found at http://www.oecd.org/pisa/.
3. Pearson, which defines itself as "The World's learning Company," publishes annual reports on the "efficacy" of its products and services. https://www.pearson.com/corporate/efficacy-and-research/reports.html.
4. *Techcrunch*, the American online publication specialized in the tech industry, provides regular updates on ed techs. https://techcrunch.com.
5. M.C. Nussbaum, *The Monarchy of Fear: A Philosopher Looks at Our Political Crisis* (London and New York, NY: Simon & Schuster, 2018).
6. M.C. Nussbaum, *Creating Capabilities: The Human Development Approach* (Cambridge, MA: Harvard University Press, 2013).

7. M.C. Nussbaum, *From Disgust to Humanity: Sexual Orientation and Constitutional Law* (Oxford and New York, NY: Oxford University Press, 2010).
8. The Wolfenden Report led to a historical debate between H.L.A. Hart, then professor of Jurisprudence at the University of Oxford, and Lord Devlin. See H.L.A. Hart, *Law, Liberty and Morality (Henry Camp Lectures at Stanford University)* (Oxford: Oxford University Press, 1963).
9. This statement is known as the "Harm Principle". J.S. Mill, *On Liberty* (London: Penguin, 2010); p. 8.
10. For an extensive analysis of moral and legal paternalism, see K. Grill and J. Hanna (eds.), *The Routledge Handbook of the Philosophy of Paternalism* (London and New York, NY: Routledge).
11. M.C. Nussbaum, *Not for Profit: Why Democracy Needs the Humanities* (Princeton, NJ and Woodstock, UK: Princeton University Press, 2010); Kindle ed., loc. 165. And *Cultivating Humanity: A Classical Defense of Reform in Liberal Education* (London and Cambridge, MA: Harvard University Press, 1997); Epilogue: *The "New" Liberal Education.*
12. S. Hartley, *The Fuzzy and the Techie: Why the Liberal Arts Will Rule the Digital World* (Boston and New York, NY: Houghton Mifflin Harcourt, 2017); pp. 5–6.
13. Ibid., p. 5.
14. Ibid., p. 7.
15. Ibid., p. 205.
16. S. Iniguez de Onzono, *Cosmopolitan Managers. Executive Education That Works* (London: Palgrave Macmillan, 2016); Kindle ed., loc. 2815.
17. W.R. Scott, *Institutions and Organizations* (Los Angeles, CA: Sage, 1995); p. 33.
18. S. Goshal, Bad Management Theories Are Destroying Good Management Practices, 4 *Academy of Management Learning & Education* (2005), 75–91.
19. Ibid.
20. Ibid.
21. Ibid.
22. H. Mintzberg, *Managers Not MBAs: A Hard Look at the Soft Practice of Managing and Management Practice* (San Francisco, CA: Berrett-Koehler Publishers Inc., 2004).
23. Quoted in Scott Hartley, *The Fuzzy and the Techie: Why the Liberal Arts Will Rule the Digital World*, op. cit., p. 14.

8

Fortitude: Hannah Arendt/Maria Tereza Leme Fleury

Fair, Fearless, Forerunner: Tereza Fleury[1]

BRICS, the acronym coined two decades ago by economist Jim O'Neill to describe five fast-growing economies with huge geopolitical potential: Brazil, Russia, India, China and South Africa,[2] immediately caught the business world's imagination and was soon the topic of innumerable conferences and forums around the world.

In line with this interest in the new global players, in 2009 one of the key business schools' conferences included a panel made up of deans from BRICS countries. Maria Tereza Fleury, then dean of EAESP Fundação Getulio Vargas, in Sao Paulo, Brazil, remembers the occasion well. She expressed the views of many other representatives of emerging economies when she said: "We don't want to be providers of business schools in developed countries; we want to be partners." Partners, not providers, became the leitmotiv of the conference and was echoed in other presentations.

Fleury's proposition is legitimate and reflects the aspirations of businesses and organizations in emerging economies that want to open up to globalization and are looking for equitable relationships with their partners, reciprocity, a shared vision and a fair distribution of profits. This is also often the response to multinationals looking to enter emerging economies guilty of a colonialist attitude. The same applies to education. For example, when I talk to journalists outside Europe and I'm asked if the institution I represent, IE University, intends to open a campus outside Europe, I tend to reply that our preferred strategy is to develop activities in other countries on a partnership basis, because those universities will have a better understanding and knowledge of the local market. Education is a culturally sensitive area, as well as one subject to all kinds of local regulations and restrictions.

My experience has shown that a good number of academic directors are outliers in terms of their profile and career. When Fleury was appointed dean of Sao Paulo University's business school, she didn't seem the most likely choice: She was a woman, and, sadly, barely 30% of faculty in the top business schools are female.

During her career as an academic director, Fleury has given special importance to the nature of the institutions where she has worked, their mission and their values: "I think that each institution has its own values, which are often strong and shared, and the manager who leads the institution needs to hold values aligned with the institution, since you have to believe in what you are doing.

> I was very lucky to be able to lead two very important business schools in Brazil, first a public business school, at University of Sao Paulo, with a very different governance style from the privately run FGV I led afterwards. In both cases I had to discuss and negotiate the agenda with peers, mobilize resources, formulate the strategy, and foster its implementation. Unless you feel a strong sense of identity and share the values of your institution all those challenges become unbearable."

Fleury believes in the power of education to transform a society: "Education is decisive for a country's development; business schools can play a big role preparing the next generation of leaders.

> I led a group of colleagues who created the first MBA program at the University of Sao Paulo, because we wanted to prepare the next generations to face the challenges of the 1990s and the beginning of the new century. And I think somehow, we made difference, because we were pioneers. We also implemented a quota system giving preference to students from public, rather than private schools. This helped the inclusion not only of females but also of minorities"

During her mandate as dean of FGV, Fleury consolidated the school's international presence. I have met her at several forums and networking events, from the OECD annual conference in Paris, to the Academy of International Business meeting, which I have chaired. She is a tireless presence on panels, running conferences, participating in committees and boards, as well as meeting one-on-one with colleagues. She is multifaceted, able to move easily from research to management, taking part in a range of forums where she interacts with the most relevant stakeholders in the academic and business worlds. This ability to be not just a generator of knowledge, a guru, but also an academic leader in every sense makes her what I like to call a kangaroo, adept at leaping from one activity to another and performing equally well in all.

Fleury is an optimist by nature, despite the challenges facing the world, and her own country. She is currently teaching a course on International Business, addressing the problems raised by the trade war between China and the United States, in which she believes the EU could play a role as mediator.

She believes that technology means global integration an irreversible process, making the role of government and multilateral organizations is particularly relevant in supervising and creating regulations and controls to promote innovation and sustainability. Brazil will be important in agriculture, she says, but the Amazon must be protected for the good of the planet.

At a meeting in Brighton in 2019 organized by the University of Sussex, she says she was struck by how sad and nostalgic one of her colleagues was as he told her he was writing a book for his descendants about how the world is heading for annihilation. For her part, Fleury says were she to write a book for her grandchildren, she would try to come up with something positive, emphasizing all the good things that have been achieved, as well as what can still be done. "We have to prepare the new generations promoting diversity, promoting inclusion, and changing the mindset of the Brazilian leaders as regards the people who come from different parts of the country, people with different backgrounds, gender, and status.

> I believe that we can help to transform the mindset of this new generation and prepare them to be more entrepreneurial, more socially committed and open to new opportunities in technology. We have to prepare them for this new scenario with careers spanning 50 years and that will change many times. At the same time, while we try to instill ethical values in our students, we know that what's happening in the business world is not setting a good example. We have to reinforce ethics constantly."[3]

Fleury says that she has been fortunate to have been supported at key moments over her career, highlighting the mentorship of Ruth Cardoso, Professor of Anthropology at the University of Sao Paulo, social entrepreneur and the wife of Fernando Henrique Cardoso, a former president of Brazil. Ruth Cardoso was behind the creation of the Bolsa Familia, the social welfare program introduced by President Lula da Silva in 2003. Cardoso was due to accompany Fleury at her inauguration as dean of FGV in 2008, but died a few days before.

As a sociologist, Fleury is familiar with the work of Hannah Arendt and believes her ideas, while formulated in the early twentieth century, are still relevant. Arendt wrote about work, labor relations and the workplace. Fleury explains that since the last century, thinkers have done much to contribute to improving labor conditions. Taylorism was a major breakthrough in defining posts and performance. Peter Drucker's proposals for management by objectives, although initially criticized, have been implemented in many ways in most companies, while the concept of the knowledge worker has gradually replaced that of the traditional factory operative or the sales clerk. Japanese management techniques, which Fleury has also studied, have influenced the modern workplace through concepts such as quality circles, long-term employment and teamwork.

Fleury believes that labor relations and working practices will continue to be subjected to rapid change, driven by the development of new technologies. She cites the example of an event shortly before we spoke, in July 2019, when truck drivers went on strike and blockaded roads and ports, bringing the country to a standstill. Rather than through traditional union meetings, the strike was organized through social networks. "This is the way that social movements now organize. I believe that if Hannah Arendt were alive, she would be very active on social media" concludes Fleury.

A Critical Thinker During Critical Times: Hannah Arendt

Some people's lives capture our imagination for their intensity and totality, their passion, their authenticity and commitment, and not least for their legacy. Hannah Arendt is one such case: dynamic, an intellectual beacon, a woman of ideas and action. Born into an intellectual German-Jewish family in the early years of the twentieth century, she was a precocious student growing up in Königsberg, modern-day Kaliningrad, Immanuel Kant's birthplace and where he spent his entire life, saying of it: "Such a town is the right place for gaining knowledge concerning men and the world, even without traveling."[4]

Arendt ignored Kant's advice to stay put and as a result, her life would be anything but contemplative, the ideal she outlined in *The Human Condition,* drawing on the ideas of Plato for a life that established a better understanding of the world of ideas and that would provide objective vision. Instead, she chose the alternative, active life he also described, one that requires interaction with other people and on which social institutions are built and political decisions made.

Arendt even rejected the term philosopher, preferring to see herself as a political theorist, with its practical connotations.[5] She studied at the University of Marburg with Martin Heidegger, whose ideas influenced her early thinking, among others that "thinking is an activity," that ideas are not just speculation or concepts to be pondered over but that can transform the world. Arendt wrote of "passionate thinking," an attitude she maintained throughout her career, in defense of ideas and political choices. She had a relationship with Heidegger, who was married with two children, and which only came to light after the publication of his letters in 1995, when both were dead. Heidegger would support the Nazi party after it came to power in 1933, appointing him rector of the University of Freiburg. After World War II, Arendt would attempt to justify Heidegger's decision, saying he had been used by Hitler and that he was never a Nazi. In a 1971 letter to him, she wrote: "You are the first to know that there is no one else like you."[6]

In the late 1920s, after leaving Marburg, she studied at Freiburg, where she attended courses by Edmund Husserl, and then at Heidelberg, where she met Karl Jaspers, with whom she would maintain a friendship and intellectual exchange throughout her life. Her doctoral thesis dealt with the concept of love in the work of Saint Augustine. During this time, she met her first husband, Günther Stern, a sociologist.

Arendt's biographers highlight her relative luck during the first months of the Nazi regime[7]: She was arrested by the Gestapo in early 1933 after writing a piece on Nazi anti-Zionist propaganda, but was released after a few days. Within months, she and her mother had fled to Paris, and for the next seventeen years, she would be stateless until she obtained US citizenship in 1951. Her lengthy status as a refugee would influence her thinking and is reflected in some of her work. She had already noticed the growing numbers of refugees and stateless persons created after World War I and the collapse of the European empires, people whose constitutional and legal identity was identified with a specific culture, language and traditions.

This phenomenon has continued ever since, and in recent decades, the emergence of new conflicts and crises has prompted further migratory flows from Africa and the Middle East into Europe and from Latin America to the United States and Canada. Migration is an uncomfortable topic that most people acknowledge, but few embrace seriously.

In Paris, Arendt met her second husband, fellow German Heinrich Blücher, a member of the Communist Party. During her six years in the

French capital she was active in Zionist circles, until in May 1940, ahead of the German invasion, the French authorities began rounding up "enemy aliens" and she was sent to the Gurs prison camp in the south of the country, but she managed to escape through Spain and Portugal and on to the United States. This odyssey reflected her combative spirit, resilience and commitment to fighting injustice.

Once in the United States, she first learned English and then began writing and lecturing. She would be appointed Princeton University's first female full professor in 1959, as well as teaching at the University of Chicago and The New School for Social Research in New York. She remained active politically and spoke out publicly against the anti-communist witch hunts led by Joseph McCarthy, as well as writing in favor of a two-state solution for Jews and Arabs, the student revolts of May of 68, the cold war and on many other issues. Perhaps seeking to make sense of her past, she wrote *The Origins of Totalitarianism*,[8] an analysis of the causes that led to the rise of the Soviet regime and Nazism, identifying the association between elites and the wider population and the use of mass propaganda and terror to establish the new regime.

In December 1974, she suffered a second heart attack and died while entertaining friends at her New York apartment, leaving her last work barely started.

The Banality of Evil

In 1960, Adolf Eichmann, one of the key men responsible for carrying out the Final Solution—the Nazi plan to kill millions of Jews in concentration camps—was kidnapped in Argentina by Israeli agents and taken to Jerusalem where he was tried for crimes against humanity. Arendt wanted to take this unique opportunity to hear at the trial, first hand, the testimony of a protagonists of one of the most evil regimes in history. She persuaded *The New Yorker* magazine to send her to cover the story, which would eventually result in her book *Eichmann in Jerusalem: A Report on the Banality of Evil*.[9]

During the Eichmann trial, the testimonies of many of the victims of the Holocaust were heard for the first time. Arendt joked about the attitude of the chief prosecutor, Gideon Hausner, whose rhetorical flourishes she felt converted the trial into a show. Never afraid of courting controversy, she also questioned the attitude of the Jewish councils throughout Europe that had worked with the Nazis, in many cases facilitating the mass deportations to the death camps.

Arendt was also struck by Eichmann's attitude during his trial, describing his composure throughout as he gave testimony, and employing the term the banality of evil, for which she is perhaps best remembered in the popular imagination:

> For when I speak of the banality of evil, I do so only on the strictly factual level, pointing to a phenomenon which stared one in the face at the trial. Eichmann was not Iago and not Macbeth, and nothing would have been farther from his mind than to determine with Richard III 'to prove a villain.' Except for an extraordinary diligence in looking out for his personal advancement, he had no motives at all... He merely, to put the matter colloquially, never realized what he was doing... It was sheer thoughtlessness — something by no means identical with stupidity —that predisposed him to become one of the greatest criminals of that period. And if this is 'banal' and even funny, if with the best will in the world one cannot extract any diabolical or demonic profundity from Eichmann, this is still far from calling it commonplace... That such remoteness from reality and such thoughtlessness can wreak more havoc than all the evil instincts taken together which, perhaps, are inherent in man — that was, in fact, the lesson one could learn in Jerusalem.[10]

Arendt's purpose was to demythologize evil, the idea that there are people somehow possessed and who have chosen the path of evil since they were children. After careful analysis of Eichmann, she concludes that evil is prosaic and that any number of ordinary people are capable of acts of great cruelty. Eichmann was not a psychopath in the conventional sense, an outcast alienated from society or suffering from a mental breakdown and therefore arguably unaccountable for his actions, but instead came over as a bureaucrat who insisted that while he was responsible for the deaths of millions of people, he was simply following orders and never personally killed anybody.

Arendt's account of the trial aroused controversy, and she was accused by some Jewish groups of portraying Eichmann sympathetically rather than focusing on his victims.[11] This was unfair, and there is no doubt that she considered Eichmann one of the worst criminals of his time. Furthermore, she fully supported the court's decision to hang him after finding him guilty.

It is nevertheless significant that Arendt chose to portray Eichmann as little more than a pen-pusher despite his having arranged the mass deportation under horrendous conditions of hundreds of thousands of human beings who he knew were then to be gassed.

After the world learnt of the crimes committed by the Nazis at the end of World War II, there was intense debate among moral philosophers on the nature of evil and the conflict between obedience and conscience. But conflict in earlier times had prompted similar discussion as to whether as humans we have an inclination either toward benevolence or evil. As mentioned above, the Geneva-born political thinker Jean-Jacques Rousseau argued in the years leading up to the French Revolution that we are born in a state of purity until our contact with society corrupts us.[12] Our only hope is return to a state of nature where we can explore our true selves. This approach was in large part inspired by the European encounter in the eighteenth century with the native peoples of the Americas and Australia who were seen by Rousseau as naive and kind, but who, once taken to the metropolis, were unable to integrate and became transgressors. The Tarzan story is inspired by this myth.

A century earlier, British philosopher Thomas Hobbes argued "*homo homini lupus*" (man is a wolf to man) and that it is only through the force of the state that we can tame our nature and guarantee relative social peace. Without the coercion of law imposed by public authorities, we would return to a natural state of chaos, where violence and the law of the strongest would prevail, making life "solitary, poor, nasty, brutish, and short."[13]

However, Arendt was not interested in generic human inclination. What she was really concerned with was how, in an advanced, educated society with collectively agreed moral principles—which the Nazi regime had still not had time to eradicate—there were still people to be found whose behavior or complicity could cause much damage, hence the banality of evil.

Shortly after Eichmann's trial, Stanley Milgram, a professor of psychology at Yale University, conducted a series of experiments that would soon be copied around the world. His original purpose was to answer the question "Could it be that Eichmann and his million accomplices in the Holocaust were just following orders? Could we call them all accomplices?"[14] Milgram selected a group of participants with different profiles he called "teachers" who were told that they had to deliver a series of electric shocks to "learners" if they did not respond correctly to a word association exercise supervised by an "experimenter" authority figure. Assigning roles was important, as we tend to associate behavior with function. The teachers were also told that the electric shocks would increase in power. In reality, no electric shocks were actually being delivered and the so-called learners, who were actors employed for the experiment, had been told to feign pain and scream louder and louder with each discharge. Had the discharges been real, by the end of the experiment, the learners would have been dead.

The main finding of the experiment was that most of the teachers followed orders, despite their protests. While all the participants eventually delivered what they believed to be 300-volt shocks to their hapless learners, 65% went all the way up to 450 volts. Milgram had conducted pre-experiment surveys with his colleagues in the psychology department who said that only 1.2% of the 100 participants would go the whole way. Based on this estimate, Milgram initially intended to carry out the experiment with Americans and then with German participants, working on the assumption that they had a more entrenched sense of duty and obedience. In view of the results with the Americans, he decided not to do the experiment with Germans. However, similar exercises in various countries have since shown that there are no significant differences in obeying authority regardless of cultural diversity.

Leaving aside the validity of comparisons between the horrors of Nazism and Milgram's disturbing experiments, the question of obedience in business is worthy of exploration, particularly in the context of how business decisions impact on the lives of others, both locally and globally. Over the course of their careers, managers are likely to receive orders or indications from above that may have harmful consequences for other people: lay-offs during a downsizing exercise, closing an unprofitable business unit, reducing expenses at the risk of lower standards or poor service, knowingly manufacturing defective products or trying to influence officials.

Critical Thinking, a Major Source of Innovation at Companies

Over the course of several conversations in the wake of the financial crisis of 2007 with Professor Paul Danos, then Dean of Tuck Business School at the University of Dartmouth, we both came to the conclusion that sometimes a kind of collective syndrome occurs within companies that prevent managers from challenging what they might see as wrong decisions and how they will also avoid contradicting their bosses, perhaps for fear of being sidelined in future promotions or being excluded from the inner circles of power. A lack of critical thinking, the failure to speak out or to contradict the established order can and have contributed to collective disaster.

Many of the mistakes that sank some financial institutions in 2007 were due to incompetent management, a failure to think critically and to objectively analyze key decisions, rather than a simple absence of ethics. What was missing during the boom years was any kind of professional deontology, which requires managers to apply extreme caution when carrying out risk assessment and decision-making. While there seemed to be no intention to deliberately cause evil in the heady days of the late 1990s and early

2000s, many people were spellbound by the illusion of unlimited economic growth, coupled with an aberrant concept of financial risk, which is not to say that the men and women involved are in any way exempt from responsibility.

A saying that has become the golden rule for many employees is "the boss is always right." Wrong. I believe that business schools have a duty to teach our students that professional ethics, best practice and fiduciary duty, on behalf of the shareholders, are for managers to use their better judgment to explore the best decision in the face of any business dilemma, even if it means contradicting the boss. Whenever friends or students ask me about the best way to act in such cases, I always make the same recommendation: *Express the highest respect for your boss, but say what you really think, stating the reasons that justify your opinion: that's what they pay you for.*

That said, I should add that I understand the unquestioning attitude of many managers, even when they know the boss is wrong. Most of the participants in Milgram's experiment did what they were told, regardless of their doubts, and their job was not at stake. Nevertheless, anybody who aspires to leadership must rise to the occasion and say what they think in a difficult situation, regardless of the risk. Good bosses will always appreciate critical, respectful and constructive judgment from their subordinates. If they don't, then perhaps they are not somebody worth working for.

The first beneficiaries of critical thinking in companies are the bosses. Complacence and resistance to rethinking ideas, processes and activities is the beginning of a slippery slope that can ruin a company. All bosses want their ideas to be supported, particularly by their subordinates, and criticism or opposition is unlikely to be well received. But good bosses are prepared to develop the capacity to listen and value criticism: It provides a good opportunity to innovate and improve the company's performance. Needless to say, any debate must not imply inaction or delay in decision-making. A balance is required between discussion and speedy implementation of decisions.

Fostering a critical spirit among senior managers, encouraging constructive debate, drives innovation and better practice, which in turn improve the bottom line, argues Helen Lee Bouygues, President of the Reboot Foundation. She recommends three courses of action to boost this capacity in organizations.[15]

— The first is to systematically question the assumptions that inform the company's strategy and fundamental decisions while at the same time avoiding throwing the baby out with the bathwater. Some assumptions are part of the company's knowledge pool and have been acquired

through experience, making them valuable rules worth following. In any event, even if these assumptions are respected, there is no harm in reviewing them periodically. Times change and some sectors experience the entry of disruptive competitors that can dramatically transform the rules of the game.
– Second, reason through logic, based on the relevant information and reasonable arguments that can convince our stakeholders. There are two fundamental factors to take into account here. The first is an excess of information. Paradoxically, big data has not made it any easier to make important decisions in business. In many cases, too much information can lead to errors in decision-making. The second factor is overestimating the opinions of experts, external consultants or senior management, whose views tend to carry more weight. This is not necessarily a bad thing: Experience is the mother of science. At the same time, fresh input often provides an opportunity for improvement.
– Third, Bouygues recommends managers to seek out diversity of thought and collaboration. Most studies confirm our intuition: Diversity, well managed, generates greater opportunities for innovation.

As I said before, the spiral of unethical behavior in a company, on a collective scale, is usually a process rather than the result of a single action or decision. As Andrew Hill, Management Editor at the *Financial Times*, explains: "Bad outcomes often result from many small steps, not single reckless leaps. The Enron board's notorious decision to waive its code of conduct and allow its chief financial officer to serve as general partner for an off-balance-sheet vehicle was the culmination of a series of smaller decisions. Directors were led step by step into the mire." Hill adds that "bad culture starts at the top." There are only two reasons for widespread unethical behavior in a company: Senior management is either leading it, or if it isn't, then it's incompetent and should be replaced.[16]

Takeaways

As a philosopher and political theorist, Arendt covered a wide range of areas, both speculative and applied. In this chapter, we have focused principally on two: her analysis of the nature of evil, based on her work of the trial of leading Nazi Adolf Eichmann in 1961 and the need to develop our critical sensibilities not just to be able to confront injustice in society, but also in the workplace. These are the conclusions of that analysis.

- Evil happens. In general, humans are neither saints nor devils, but circumstances can lead, typically after a series of bad decisions to further decisions with evil or criminal consequences. One way to prevent this happening is to exercise our critical sensibilities, to express our opinion when we believe that what is taking place is wrong or mistaken.
- Many people are prepared to unquestioningly accept the maxim "the boss is always right." But we should remember that the best leaders try to surround themselves with people who are more intelligent than themselves, people able to say what they think, regardless of the consequences. If we don't say what we think to our superiors, even if it means contradicting them, then we are not behaving ethically, and will not be meeting our boss's expectations either.
- In order to develop the ability to make constructive criticism at work, we need to question the validity of our ideas and arguments periodically. What's more, encouraging diversity of all kinds in our teams is healthy for creativity and innovation.

Notes

1. The quotes in this section are extracted from an interview between Maria Tereza Fleury and the author in Sao Paulo, on August 19, 2020.
2. J. O'Neill, Building Better Economic BRICs, *Goldman Sachs Global Economics Paper*, no. 66, November 30, 2001. https://www.goldmansachs.com/insights/archive/archive-pdfs/build-better-brics.pdf.
3. Stella Campos, Careers Editor at Valor, the business and economy publication of Globo, the Brazilian media conglomerate, publishes annual surveys of the evolution of women in leadership positions in Brazilian companies. See, for example: https://valor.globo.com/carreira/mercado-executivo/coluna/mulheres-em-cargos-de-lideranca-aumentam-o-lucro-das-empresas-na-al.ghtml.
4. Quoted in E. Young-Bruehl, *Hannah Arendt. For Love of the World* (New Haven, CT, and London: Yale University Press, 1982); p. 5.
5. M. Betz Hull, *The Hidden Philosophy of Hannah Arendt* (London and New York, NY: RoutledgeCurzon, 2002); p. 1.
6. H. Saña Herrero, *Atlas of Universal Thought* (Córdoba: Almuzara, 2008); p. 303.
7. L. Adler, *Hannah Arendt: Una biografía*, I. Margelí (trans.) (Barcelona: Ariel, 2019); Ch. 3.
8. H. Arendt, *The Origins of Totalitarianism* (New York, NY: Houghton Miffin Harcourt, 1951).

9. H. Arendt; *Eichmann in Jerusalem*, A. Elon (introd.) (London and New York, NY: Penguin, 1964).
10. R. Bernstein, *Why Read Hannah Arendt Today?*, Spanish ed. (Madrid: Gedisa, 1999); Kindle ed., p. 418.
11. L. Adler, *Hannah Arendt, una biografía*, op. cit., Ch. XIV.
12. J.J. Rousseau, *Discourse on Political Economy and the Social Contract*, C. Batts (trans.) (Oxford and New York, NY: Oxford University Press, 2008).
13. T. Hobbes, *Leviathan* (Oxford and New York, NY: Oxford University Press, 2008); I, xiii, 9.
14. S. Milgram, *Obedience to Authority: An Experimental View* (New York, NY: HarperCollins, 1974).
15. H. Lee Bouygues, Simple Habits to Improve Your Critical Thinking, *Harvard Business Review*, May 6, 2019. https://hbr.org/2019/05/3-simple-habits-to-improve-your-critical-thinking.
16. A. Hill, Ten Years on, Enron Remains an Open Sore. The Real Lessons Went Unheeded, *Financial Times*, October 17, 2011. https://www.ft.com/content/9d57f8da-f66d-11e0-86dc-00144feab49a.

9

Passion: Simone Weil/Michelle Raymond

Per aspera ad astra: Michelle Raymond[1]

In the old days, when going to the movies was still most people's idea of a night out, there was a strict ritual that took place after we took our seats: The red velvet curtains would slowly pull apart to reveal the huge silver screen, and then the lights would slowly dim and a hushed, expectant silence settle on the auditorium. For me, as a youngster, it was like being in a waking dream. I learned to appreciate cinema with my mother, who had a prodigious memory for names and an impressive ability to remember story lines and key scenes. At high school, for a time, I seriously considered pursuing a career in cinema: I enjoyed writing stories and imagined adapting them for the big screen. I knew several directors and producers in Spain, although in the end, I took the more conservative option of studying Law.

I've always been struck by the similarity of sitting in a darkened movie theater and Plato's allegory of the cave.[2] Movies are incomplete stories projected onto a screen, and as in Plato's cave, we see figures on the wall that are mere shadows created by a flickering light. For Plato, reality, the world of ideas, takes place outside the cave, lit by the sun, but when one of the cave dwellers goes outside and then returns to tell them the good news, he is murdered by the others, who prefer to continue watching mere copies of reality.

Cinemas, unlike caves, have a therapeutic value, offering us a way to escape or alleviate the problems we face outside, and we can imagine ourselves in the roles on screen. As David Thomson notes in *Sleeping with*

Strangers: "In the movies, as well as life, desire is contingent on things we cannot quite have. As you may have noticed, satisfaction can kill desire just as desire can make you forget your status quo."[3]

The movies can also inspire us to pursue our dreams; at least that's what Michelle "Michi" Raymond says about the 1990s comedy Sister Act. Raymond had wanted to be an artist since she was aged two and had learned several musical instruments, notably the guitar, which is now pretty much an extension of her body. She played in bars as a young woman, usually chaperoned by her parents.

At the same time, although her family was not religious, she says she felt a religious calling, and at the age of sixteen converted to Catholicism. Watching Whoopi Goldberg playing the role of a lounge singer forced to join a convent after being placed in a witness protection program and who redeems herself through music, Raymond says she found her inspiration: "Here's an artist, a rock star, who went to a convent in hiding, but I saw her develop with the children and the neighbourhood and give them something, to you know, to be excited about and develop them into these little artists, and I really connected with that, cos I was a hippy, and I felt like I didn't need material things, I was in love with this idea of sharing my music and helping other students, children that were in my area, and so, for me, I saw this movie and I felt inspired and I thought, 'OK, I'm gonna become a nun'."

Her mother nevertheless insisted that before she committed to music or the Church, she finished her education, preferably related to business, so Raymond entered Sweet Briar College, a prestigious, all-female liberal arts institution in the Blue Ridge Mountains, Virginia. Raymond says her memories of Sweet Briar are bittersweet. She finished her degree in three years, rather than four, for two reasons. On the one hand to save on the $40,000 a year tuition fees, and on the other, because she had begun a relationship with another pupil, which angered some students. On one occasion, she says her classmates refused to eat with her in the dining hall, getting up to go to another table when she joined them.

On another, she was attacked by fellow students who broke into her room and the police were called. Raymond asked for the young women not to be expelled, hoping they would learn their lesson.

"But also I didn't want to be responsible for seniors being kicked out of school for a stupid drunken mistake. Those same girls who attacked me, months later, approached me themselves and said: 'I'm really sorry, what I did was absolutely wrong, and now I realise that you never deserved that and we hope that you'll come to lunch with us and we want to apologise'. And that was like, a wow moment, that on their own, over the course of a couple of months, they came to their own realization that what happened should never have happened."

Sadly, bullying LGBTQI students is widespread in college and university. Some studies suggest that at least two-thirds of students from this collective are subjected to bullying. Homophobia and misogyny are behind this phenomenon, fed by toxic masculinity, which in turn negates femininity while stressing traditional gender roles, aptly described by sociologist C. J. Pascoe as "fag discourse." [4]

When I asked Raymond how she dealt with these situations, she said she simply focused on her work. "One thing I always did, which I would recommend to other people, is that, when I'm having this moment where the world seems against us, and I know that sounds extreme, but there are times when you feel like you don't have the peers, or you don't have anything going right.

> I would take that moment to find something that I wanted to develop and focus 100% of my energy on it, but by myself, so at that time I was struggling on academic subjects and I said: 'OK, I'm going to focus all attention into academics and cut everything else out, and if I do well here, I'm going to have a focus, I'm not going to be worried about the outside world and I'm going to do something that's going to better me', and so, I became 1000% focused on academics."

This enabled Raymond not only to resist, but also to make the Dean's List of her class and finish her studies early. She says she has happy memories of the college, particularly of a number of her teachers and the Dean, who helped her channel her creativity.

Raymond's career after graduating was in the financial services sector, and she rose to become leader of Morgan Stanley's Wealth Management pride network team, as well as working on the corporate committee of the US National Gay and Lesbian Chamber of Commerce. After ten years, she decided to take an International MBA at IE Business School, which is where I met her. During her time at our school, she transformed the reach of IE Out, the institution's LGBTQI club. She was president of the third-largest LGBTQI workplace inclusion conference organized by a business school in the world, attended by all kinds of stakeholders from around the world: students, alumni employers and influencers.

She was a much-needed breath of fresh air that strengthened IE University's diversity and inclusion: "It's very important for a leader in a business to create a culture where people aren't feeling like they're getting opportunities just because they identify in a certain way or they were born into a certain gender." She remembers that when she began running IE Out, a lot of people turned down her invitations: "They would say 'I don't want to go to your event, because people are going to think I'm gay'.

> But by the end of the year, they were the biggest allies to the group, and the biggest supporters that we had. And so you get to see this transformation because, I think things that are foreign to you are scary, but when you actually have to work with it, there's maybe this learning curve, maybe this uncomfortable moment, but people can change, and I think it's a matter of really having a hands-on experience. I could preach to you all day, but, until you actually have to work in that environment yourself, you're not truly going to learn it."

Returning to Raymond's great love, music, she remembers the first time she played in public, after a teacher to whom she will always be grateful, allowed her to perform in front of the class rather than make a traditional presentation. She played one of her own compositions and says she was very nervous. But she persevered, gradually building up her self-confidence. "Music transformed me from a shy person to a social butterfly," she says.

When she thinks about her performances, many of which are available on social networks, she realizes how her confidence has grown, saying that her experience could be useful for others who suffer from stage fright: "Now it's the complete opposite, Before it used to be a source of anxiety and now it's something I thrive on.

> I enjoy a huge audience of 200,000 people so much more than I do a room of five, because with five I know everyone's eyes are on me and I get super nervous and… but if I'm speaking at a huge event I feel so much confidence on stage; I've learnt how to read the audience, so I never make a set list, I feel how they're feeling and I adapt as I go, so if I think everyone is in a really chilled mood, and I want to bring up their energy, I'm going to play a song that has a lot of energy and see how they react, and if they react well, and they want more, I go for another higher energy song and I keep it going. But If I test the high energy song and people are more relaxed I bring it back down, something in the middle, and I'm tailoring it, the entire concert.
>
> It's really like reading the audience and seeing what they want, to give them a show that we're both going to enjoy. And then I started using those same skills from the stage to do all my presentations and business, and my speaking engagements. I'm always watching people to see if they're laughing, if they are

being honest, a look that tells me if they're into this content, or they're not understanding me, do I need a backup? Do I need it to go faster? Are they getting bored? It's always about reading people."

Comparisons, as the saying goes, are odious, and the more so between people from very different times, but when I was preparing this chapter about Simone Weil, Michi Raymond immediately came to mind. They have at least three things in common: authenticity, understood as living according to one's principles; they're both outliers, transformative and creative, belonging to no particular current; and finally, there is a certain mysticism and spirituality about them, which has meant that the objective of their lives transcends their lived experiences: philosophy for Weil and music for Raymond.

When I ask Raymond, who is still in the early stages of her career, about her long-term strategy, she replies: "My dream has always been to be an artist, and I made a very conscious decision about six months ago. Over my whole life, I've been balancing business and music, and I've gotten very far in my musical career and very far in my business career as a young person, and I always wonder, what if I focus 100% of my attention onto one thing instead of fifty/fifty? And so I made the decision, and I'm going to go for music."

She has already topped Virginia's Indie Music Charts and has opened for the likes of Miley Cyrus, DJ Marshmello, Meghan Traynor, Carly Rae Jepson and Zara Larsson. When I interviewed her in the summer of 2019, she was about to begin a Masters at Berklee School of Music, the first recipient of the Outstanding Women Scholarship and Mentorship, with Yvette Noel-Schure. I don't know in which scenario we'll see Raymond appear next, or on what online platform we'll hear her songs. What I do know is that the journey that will take her there will be fascinating.

Authenticity as Practicing What You Preach: Simone Weil

Why should managers or entrepreneurs read Marx and his disciples? Why would the business community want to study writers and thinkers who argue that history evolves through class struggle and that capitalism will perish when the proletariat seizes collective ownership of the means of production?[5]

History suggests that this goal of taking over from the ruling class is utopic and unlikely to be achieved. The states that adopted communist regimes in the last century either collapsed or have since embraced some form of capitalism. At the same time, states that still call themselves communist have little to do with the original Marxian conception. The only place where I have seen the conquest of capital by the proletariat was in a glass case that presided over the atrium of what was once the residence of the former German Democratic Republic, in Berlin's *museumsinsel*, and which, ironically enough, is now a business school.

That said, Marx may well have been right in understanding history as a series of cycles, following Hegel's conception of dialectic tensions, in which certain phenomena are repeated, such as the tensions between freedom, growth and inequality. In recent years, the debate about growing inequalities of wealth distribution, both within developed countries and on a global scale, has sparked renewed interest in Marxist philosophy, with a good number of universities reintroducing the German thinker into their curricula.[6]

I have always believed we should read not only the authors with whose thinking—what Marx would call ideology—we share an affinity, but those who challenge our principles. Ignorance is the origin of misunderstanding, hatred and irrationality. I remember that at school, a religious institution, I attended philosophy classes, and that when we reached Marx, the focus was entirely on the supposed defects of his thinking, as well as his personality: He was a hypocrite who enjoyed champagne and caviar. Or that he had been stateless most of his life—as if this were a crime for a thinker—and also neglected his family. In short, he led a bad life. In the event, we never studied Marx's ideas. In rhetoric this is often referred to as an *ad personam* attack, a criticism of the person, which is fallacious because it focuses on the personal issues of our dialectical opponents rather than discussing their ideas. It is often used in politics or informal conversation, designed to appeal to a wide audience. But in philosophy, where discussion focuses on ideas and not people, such approaches have no place.

Some people believe that philosophers must live as they think, that their principles and theories should guide their actions.[7] The subject of this chapter, Simone Weil, is an example of a woman whose life embodied her personal beliefs at the expense of health, probably leading to her early death. Framing her thinking within a particular current of thought is impossible: It is hard to know whether to categorize her as a philosopher, a mystic or simply a writer.

Her thinking connects with Plato, at the same time as reaching out to Christianity, although she also had roots in Marxism. She has inspired people as diverse as Susan Sontag, Carlos Fuentes, Pope Paul VI and Albert Camus, who compiled her work for Gallimard publishers and described her as "the only great spirit of our times."[8] She knew Trotsky and De Gaulle who, while interested in taking up her offer to work on behalf of the French government in exile, said of her, "But she is mad!".[9] Mary Warnock excluded Weil from her 1996 book *Women Philosophers* because she considered her a mystic who adhered to religious principles rather than philosophical logic.[10] In any event, she was an outlier, in life and beyond.

Weil's parents were relatively wealthy Jews who had moved to France after their native Alsace had been annexed by Germany. The couple were agnostics and encouraged their two children (Simone's brother was the mathematician André Weil) to think for themselves. Although she declared herself a Bolshevik at the age of 19, Weil had been attracted to Christianity from a young age, particularly the mysteries of the crucifixion and transubstantiation. She recounts three mystical moments in her twenties that guided her approach to Catholicism, although she never converted. The first was during a visit to northern Portugal to recover from an accident, where she witnessed a pilgrimage by fishermen near Viana do Castelo, and was captivated by the fervor and simplicity of the worshippers. The second came in 1937 at the spectacular Romanesque chapel of Santa Maria degli Angeli in Assisi, Italy, where she described experiencing a religious ecstasy. The following year, at the Benedictine abbey of Solesmes, during Holy Week, the combination of Gregorian chant and the work of the 17th English metaphysical poet George Herbert led her to write "Christ himself came down and took me."[11]

Weil's life goes beyond commitment and verges on martyrdom, although it is not easy to understand the motives for her sense of sacrifice. Perhaps the two most extreme moments of her experience, seen by some as heroic, were her decision to work on the assembly line at a Renault factory until she succumbed to exhaustion and then to join the anarchists of Buenaventura Durruti in fighting the nationalist forces of General Francisco Franco during the Spanish Civil War (1936–1939). Aside from her extreme shortsightedness, which apparently made her a danger to her fellow soldiers, she was deeply disillusioned by an event during which militiamen shot a young nationalist soldier who had refused to join their ranks. Eventually, she was persuaded to abandon the struggle and her parents, who had followed her to Spain, took her back to France, leading some critics to suggest that her exposure to risk was not as reckless as it seemed.[12]

The circumstances of Weil's death at the age of 34 are still unclear. She had been diagnosed with tuberculosis, but had refused to rest and continued trying to find a way to be sent as an undercover agent to France. In solidarity, she had limited her diet to the rations imposed by the Germans on the French population. She was admitted to a sanatorium in Ashford, Kent, in the summer of 1943, but within a few weeks, perhaps weakened by voluntary starvation, she died.

Work: Alienation or Liberation?

As mentioned, in 1934, Weil decided to give up her position as a high school philosophy teacher in rural France and keen to better understand the reality of working-class industrial life, took a job on the assembly line at a Renault factory. Unprepared for the tough conditions, she found the work physically exhausting but spiritually rewarding, and formed friendships with her workmates, who helped her as she struggled to learn the job.

Few philosophers have turned their attention to the subject of work, at least with the same level of detail as other related phenomena of human activity, such as technology. Generally, a philosophy of work refers to the values and principles we bring to our jobs, and the way work is organized and implemented, rather than the role work plays in our development or in the attainment of human happiness.

Some philosophers have explored work from a collective perspective, as one of the factors of production. Jean-Paul Sartre argued that the "golden age of work for philosophy" was due to the "tenacious presence, from my viewpoint, of the working masses, that huge and grim body that lived Marxism."[13] Weil also criticized the lack of interest in the topic in classical philosophy: "A philosophy work has yet to be created. It is perhaps indispensable. It is perhaps more particularly needed in this age." She added: "Art / science / work / philosophy first. Plato said no more than half."[14]

The evolution of the labor market, the transformation of the industrial economy into a knowledge economy, as well as the rise of freelancers and entrepreneurship, among other factors, may make talk of the "working class" sound anachronistic. Labor unions still have a presence in some countries, but their political influence has largely waned. As Robert Chenavier, author of *Attention to the Real*, a study of Weil's work, argues, "From André Gorz's *Farewell to the Working Class* (1980) to *The End of Work*, by Jeremy Rifkin (1996) through to Dominique Méda's *Le travail, une valeur in voie of disparition* (1995) it would be hard to keep up with the reasons to give up on the philosophical reflection of work."[15]

Weil wanted to go beyond Marx's materialism, which sees work as a source of alienation, although her quasi-religious approach is somewhat cryptic. She explains that materialism cannot be understood without a spiritual facet: "There is no thought and work; work is no less thought than reflection. It is nothing less than an absolute act of the spirit."[16] On the other hand, she explains how in ancient times those who performed most of the work, except for waging war, were slaves and servants. Christianity, in its mystical vision, is a religion of slaves, in which Christ himself becomes a slave, which is why Weil rejects the idea of work as alienating.[17] At the same time, her defense of manual labor over other work is puzzling. Perhaps her mysticism or her own difficulties in performing the hard physical tasks at the Renault factory produced a certain complex that led her to downplay intellectual work, which she excelled at.

Weil's limited experience in heavy industry nevertheless allowed her to formulate a vision of work that is still relevant today. I am interested in two of her ideas in particular. The first is sustainability in business. Weil discussed the risks of overproduction resulting from the development of technology: "Automatic machines only offer advantages to the extent that they are used to produce in series and in bulk quantities; [...] they offer the temptation to produce much more than is necessary to meet real needs, which leads to spending, to no benefit, a great wealth of human strength and raw materials."[18]

Marx argued that the returns on labor under a socialist system would generate sufficient wealth for equal redistribution. In his view, it was capital that prevented the full development of productive forces. Weil did not share this vision, dismissing it as illusory and impracticable, and instead proposes two major lines of action to improve the development of business that would better the wellbeing of the masses.

Firstly, the rationalization of work. We should remember that Weil took part in the early stages of Taylorism, the introduction of new technology and assembly methods in factories to improve productivity. Antonio Gramsci, the Italian communist philosopher and a contemporary of Weil, referred to this process of specialization and increased productivity as Fordism (in reference to the Ford car company, which pioneered assembly lines), explaining that the rise of the new specialized operator marks the transition of the proletariat toward the creation of a middle class "the American way."

The second initiative is the development of technology, of new machines, to use the terminology of her time, as well as of new sources of power. Weil refers to the two energy sources used in factories, coal and heavy oils. Thinking ahead of her time, she suggests the need to use other energies she calls natural, even if they entail higher costs, to improve conditions for workers and society overall.

Weil's contribution remains relevant given our unease at the growing automation of so many activities previously implemented by humans. Any number of studies suggest that in the coming decades many jobs and trades will disappear, especially those of a routine nature that can be performed more quickly and without errors by robots or algorithms.

There are two main visions of where this will lead. The first is dystopian, a world dominated by technology, where robots, replicators and cyborgs emerge the victors of the fourth industrial revolution at the expense of an enslaved humanity. A number of important figures have warned of the dangers we face in this regard, such as Stephen Hawking, Bill Gates and Elon Musk, but I see little reason for such concerns. It will be some time before artificial intelligence and other technologies are sufficiently sophisticated to represent any threat to us, and along the way, new opportunities will emerge we cannot imagine at the moment.

By the same token, there are some tasks that should remain the preserve of humanity. Most of us would prefer to see humans continue in their posts as judges, teachers, the clergy and managers, even if they sometimes make mistakes; surely the risk of human error is more acceptable than the fear of an arbitrary decision of a robot.

The second vision of our where automation and AI are taking us is utopian. Most socialist thinkers qualify as utopian and propose models of society where the aspirations of justice, equality and freedom have been fulfilled and we live in peaceful coexistence, while resources are shared equally.

While we are still waiting for this utopia, the development of technology, artificial intelligence and, in parallel, of neurobiology, medicine and cognitive psychology, all working in conjunction with other sciences and the Humanities, offers a better future.

Will Education Become Fully Automatized?

A field where many visionaries envision profound transformations by AI and machine learning in the future is education. Imagine, for a moment, that a device I will call the Educatron offers the following wonderful possibilities to its user. The Educatron has archived all the knowledge stored in the most important libraries in the world. In addition, it has the capacity to process all the most relevant data on a particular profession, area of knowledge, physical or intellectual skill. When a person enters this machine, connecting different areas of the body, including the brain, via electrodes to the Educatron, they can download all the knowledge generated by humanity and artificial intelligence within five minutes. And for good measure, the Educatron can also program the body to be able to practice any sport.

Who wouldn't want to use the Educatron to achieve their dreams?

When I have asked this question in my lectures, I never fail to be surprised that so few people raise their hands. My next question is why wouldn't we want to be hooked up to this marvelous machine?

In my opinion, education is a journey: It is what we learn along the way to acquiring knowledge that is important, the process of learning in itself. The reason we enjoy engaging in a particular activity is closely linked to the process by which we acquired the ability to do so, as well as the effort used to practice it with skill. The happiness and enjoyment of learning something, or of acquiring a capacity, are not only in achieving it, but in the process, the path we travel along to achieve it. This is the central idea behind Homer's *Odyssey*, which tells the story of the journey our Greek hero undertakes before finally arriving in Ithaca, his homeland. What gives meaning to his life is not arriving home and sorting out his family affairs after many years of travel, but all the episodes he has experienced, the encounters with so many characters, how much he learned and internalized during the journey.

Weil seems to share this belief. In addition to being an expert in Homer's work and having written about *The Iliad*, the intensity of her own life and her interest in experiencing multiple experiences reflect a spirit similar to that of Ulysses. Far from being satisfied with learning things quickly or knowing life through books, she wanted to gain experience firsthand, without help and without anesthesia.

Takeaways

How realistic is it to try to practice what we preach?

- Authenticity has attracted a lot of attention in management literature in recent years and is seen as an attribute closely linked to leadership and being able to motivate others.[19] Simone Weil's belief in living her life according to her principles resulted in an early death. She was an outlier in her approach, which some have described as quasi-mystical, although she also connected with a diverse range of thinkers, from Plato to Marx.
- Work was traditionally been seen as a less worthy activity that religious or mystical contemplation within Christianity, at least until the rise of Protestantism, with its work ethic, and that related success with the spirit

of capitalism, according to Max Weber.[20] For Marx, work was a form of alienation. One of the merits of Weil's philosophy was to raise the need for a philosophy of work: Can work be transcendent and can we make work a more dignified activity?
- Weil's vision of the future of work was pioneering, and some of her efforts to rationalize it were later developed in management studies and Taylorism, along with the replacement of routine activities through automation. She also foresaw the phenomenon of sustainability, calling for coal to be replaced with renewable sources of energy. Weil was a visionary, a woman ahead of her times.

Notes

1. In Latin: "through hardship to the stars," a motto adopted by several educational institutions, noble families and other organizations. The quotes in this section were extracted from an interview between Michelle Raymond and the author in Madrid, on September 6, 2019.
2. Plato, *The Republic*, R. Waterfield (trans.) (Oxford and New York, NY: Oxford University Press, 2008); pp. 514a–520a.
3. D. Thomson, *Sleeping with Strangers* (New York, NY: Knopf Doubleday Publishing Group, 2019); p. 10.
4. C.J. Pascoe, *Dude You're a Fag: Masculinity and Sexuality in High School* (Berkeley, Los Angeles, and London: University of California Press, 2011).
5. K. Marx and F. Engels, *The Communist Manifesto*, D. McLellan (ed.) (Oxford and New York, NY: Oxford University Press, 2008); *Capital*, D. McLellan (ed.) (Oxford and New York, NY: Oxford University Press, 2008).
6. S. Jeffries, Why Marxism Is on the Rise Again, *The Guardian*, July 4, 2012. https://www.theguardian.com/world/2012/jul/04/the-return-of-marxism.
7. See, for example, J. Miller, *Examined Lives: From Socrates to Nietzsche* (New York, NY: Farrar, Straus and Giroux, 2011).
8. A. Camus, El hombre rebelde, in *Obras Completas* (México DF: Aguilar, 1973); p. 704.
9. Palle Yourgrau, *Simone Weil (Critical Lives)* (p. 98). Reaktion Books. Kindle ed.
10. "I have… omitted", wrote the editor, Mary Warnock, a distinguished philosopher in her own right, in the book's introduction "the writings of women who, to put it crudely, seem to rely more on dogma, revelation or mystical experience than on argument." M. Warnock (ed.), *Women Philosophers* (London: J.M. Dent, 1998).
11. E. Bea (ed.), *Simone Weil. La conciencia del dolor y de la belleza* (Madrid: Trotta, 2010), Kindle ed., loc. 226.

12. J.R. Capella, Pensamiento sin orden sobre la existencia de Simone Weil, in E. Bea (ed.), *Simone Weil. La conciencia del dolor y de la belleza*, op. cit., Kindle ed., loc. 2530.
13. E. Bea, *Simone Weil. La conciencia del dolor y de la belleza*, op. cit., Kindle ed., loc. 3283–3285.
14. Ibid., Kindle ed., loc. 3289–3293.
15. Ibid.
16. S. Weil, *Oeuvres Complètes* (Paris: Gallimard, 1988); Vol. I, p. 378.
17. S. Weil, *A la espera de Dios*, M. Tabuyo and A. López (trans.) (Madrid: Trotta, 2018); p. 40.
18. S. Weil, *Reflexiones sobre las causas de la libertad y de la opresión social*, C. Revilla (trans.) (Barcelona: Paidós, 1995); pp. 62–63.
19. D. Weinberger, Authenticity: Is It Real or Is It Marketing? *Harvard Business Review*, March 2008.
20. M. Weber, *The Protestant Ethic and the Spirit of Capitalism*, Talcott Parsons (trans.) (New York, NY: Routledge, 2005).

10

Ethics: Adela Cortina/Inés Temple

Reflecting on the Enterprise of One's Life: Inés Temple[1]

Whether we like it or not, it's a sure bet that most people going into management will, over the course of their careers, change companies, positions, and maybe even sectors. Why? For two reasons: We're living longer, which means we're going to be working longer; and because of the impact of technology on the labor market, which will require us to constantly adapt and to learn new skills and knowledge.

Each year, I teach a course in Competitive Strategy to a group of Executive MBA students made up of professionals from a range of countries, typically with at least a decade's management experience behind them. In one of the sessions, dealing with growth strategies, I ask them how many mergers and acquisitions (M&A) they have been involved in. Over the years, I have noticed how the average number of my executive students who have experienced three or more M&As has risen to around 60%, due, I would venture, to the globalization of a growing number of sectors.

While this evidence is largely anecdotal, I believe it gives an idea of the dynamism that now characterizes many sectors, and that as we will likely experience a merger or buy out at some point in our career, we had better be ready. Mergers tend to mean layoffs for directors, given that the idea is usually to reduce costs and improve efficiency. That said, as experience and research show, this doesn't always happen automatically. One study shows that the majority of layoffs have little, or even a negative, impact on the bottom line and market value of the company.[2]

For most of us, being laid off will come as an unpleasant surprise, leaving us feeling hard done by. What's more, this tends to coincide with the dreaded mid-career crisis,[3] which can escalate into a full-blown personal crisis unless we strengthen our ability to deal with adversity as well as being ready to use the services of a coach and learn new skills.

Being laid off may be an unwelcome surprise, but it can also be an opportunity to take your career in a new direction and develop additional skills. In 1993, after her husband's layoff was handled unprofessionally and insensitively, Inés Temple read an article in New York University's alumni magazine about outplacement: "A service that helps companies manage the way they handle professional change.

> Processes of change that are managed competently, when they involve the departure of people, in a respectful, human, considerate manner, making sure that the people leaving are treated with the maximum respect and care for their self-esteem, identity and dignity."

Since then, outplacement and coaching and the relationship with hundreds of directors that have changed company or job, has become the professional passion and recognized forte of Temple, Executive President of LHH-DBM Peru and President of the Board of LHH Chile, the leading companies in outplacement and talent development in both countries.

Temple is also regarded as the most influential director in Peru, publishing columns and articles in media such as *El Comercio*, the country's leading daily, as well as blogs and her YouTube channel, which has attracted some 5.5 million views. In recent years, she has expanded her activities to other sectors, such as storage, and in other countries, such as the United States. Her bestseller, *You Inc*,[4] is a guide for directors to improve their employability. As she explains in the book, her personal experience has taught her that we live in fast-changing times and that working for a large organization is no longer a guarantee of job for life.

Her approach is to exchange the assurance once invested in organizations, the expectation of a career spent working for a single employer, into self-assurance in oneself: "We are closer than ever to achieving that utopia of the ideal job in so much as we can build and strengthen our own career and work toward our own competitiveness, making us more attractive for businesses and employers."[5]

The guarantee for remaining competitive is employability, "the paradigm of our working life. Building it, developing it and demonstrating it is our permanent task." Temple defines employability as "the capacity to add value and develop the skills required to find or maintain a space to contribute professionally in (that's to say, clients for my services), when and where necessary."[6]

Temple sees employability as a long-term challenge, which has to be worked on throughout a career, and is optimistic about the future. She believes that we are at the mid-way point in our life at the age of sixty: "I see myself as being in the middle of my life. I am interested in everything that has to do with technology and education, and I'm curious about the phenomenon of longevity and what the experts have to say about it. It seems that if we take care of ourselves, and the advance of science, it's possible that we'll live many more years than before.

> Therefore, I have the desire, the disposition, the energy, and I'm at that moment in life when I have the freedom to continue growing, to know other cultures, other places, to learn other languages. I feel I have found the energy I had at the age of 35, the desire to set up new companies, to enter new markets, to offer something, and above all, to feel relevant. I don't like the idea of being left behind, of not being, of not having anything to offer. I am in the next stage of my life, creating my strategy; what to do so as to keep evolving, thinking about who I make connections with, so that my territories expand and that my message, which is simple but powerful, can reach more people who need it now, more than ever."

Temple explains her attitude of being permanently employable by comparing the career of a director and a company's activities. An impactful career requires a strategy, a long-term approach, good financial management, anticipating the resources required to invest in development and training, and of course marketing and networking. Temple highlights the importance of emotional and interpersonal skills, and not just intellectual and technical abilities. This is consistent with what other outsourcing experts recommend when they talk about honoring people in personal relationships as a way of guaranteeing permanent employability.[7]

Temple believes that the two most important qualities for a CEO are a passion for their activity and, most importantly, integrity, ethical behavior. As she explains, "everything one says or does is now recorded by the digital media, which encourages us to rethink how we did things before, when weren't exposed in this way.

> Ethics are intrinsic to each of us, to being human, to who we are, our education and upbringing, what we believe in, our consciousness, how we have evolved. Nevertheless, I also believe that applying marketing concepts, personal branding to ethics, helps many people to understand its importance from a pragmatic perspective: Look, we have to act properly because it's not just morally right, but it's the only way to manage our career in the long term, because every good thing you do will always be known, and your reputation, your personal brand will be associated with what you do, your behavior, today, tomorrow, and thirty years ago.
>
> Sometimes in Latin America, we've believed in impunity. Corrupt politicians who thinks they can get away with it. But we live in a world where it's getting harder to escape attention. In Peru, we've got four former presidents in jail, and other countries do as well. The idea is that ethics, along with talent and a reputation are the three pillars that hold up our personal brand, our degree of employability, our lifelong career. And that depends on the decisions we take and how we plan our career. That's my focus when discussing ethics."

Temple's explanation of ethical behavior in business brings to mind Immanuel Kant's distinction between the arguments for behaving prudently and those for behaving morally.[8] Arguments for behaving prudently justify an action on the basis of personal interests, for example, preserving one's reputation and good name, as Temple argues. Moral arguments, on the other hand, are those that justify an action in relation to principles that can be applied to a situation, and that in Kant's opinion, can be elevated to universal codes of conduct; for example, never paying bribes to officials.

In this chapter, we'll see two arguments for behavior, the results of which appear the same: we can avoid bribing officials for prudent reasons, although if there were no repercussions we could. But as Kant says, it's what goes on inside us that counts. Temple puts it like this: "How can you sleep at night if you're not living in accordance with your values? Furthermore, the market demands this of you today. Customers can now make themselves heard, a company's share price can go up and down based on its ethical behavior, and so this is a key subject now in terms of corporate governance and the decisions that CEOs make.

> Ostensibly, CEOs represent an organization's aims, we are the face of the company, our values are those of the company's, and we have to live them, be them, we have to be an example, we are constantly visible to the public; it's no longer just about making the right decisions, we have to be seen to be making the right decisions, particularly if we want to create a sustainable business."

Temple provides a good introduction to addressing the relationship between ethics and business, and to what extent we can propose a model of behavior or code of professional ethics for managers. Maybe, just maybe, we could see some real moral progress in our society.

Making the Connection Between Business and Ethics: Adela Cortina

Philosophers have traditionally focused their inquiries on the individual: Who am I? What can I know? How should I act? How do I relate to the world? How should I live? But the emergence of the nation-state in the nineteenth century and the rise of different political and civil entities have caught the attention of a growing number of philosophers. More recently, many have turned their attention to the phenomenon of the rise of the company, especially large corporations that not only play a major role in our economies but influence politics, drive innovation, require talent, consume resources and impact on the environment.

In short, the company is the stellar organization of our times. Ours is a managerial culture and management is all-pervasive, affecting many areas of our lives. As Peter Drucker, one of the founders of the science of management, wrote: "There are, of course, differences in management between different organizations—mission defines strategy, after all, and strategy defines structure. But the differences between managing a chain of retail stores and managing a Roman Catholic diocese are amazingly fewer than either retail executives or bishops realize." He adds:

> The differences are mainly in application rather than in principles. The executives of all these organizations spend, for instance, about the same amount of their time on people problems—and the people problems are almost always the same.
>
> So, whether you are managing a software company, a hospital, a bank or a Boy Scout organization, the differences apply to only about 10 per cent of your work. This 10 per cent is determined by the organization's specific mission, its specific culture, its specific history and its specific vocabulary. The rest is pretty much interchangeable.[9]

This recognition of companies as important social agents has had significant consequences, such as the development of laws regulating their commercial activities, how much tax they should pay or how they behave, the latter perhaps the fastest-growing area of interest. Companies and their representatives also have a growing presence in and influence over public bodies, both advisory and executive. In the United States, businesses invest in election campaigns, which might be seen as recognition of their right to freedom of expression. In Europe, the European Union and its member states have implemented legislation establishing civil and criminal liability for companies. Courts can now find companies guilty of corruption, although obviously they cannot send them to jail. As the nineteenth-century German jurist Franz von Liszt famously noted: "*Societas delinquere non potest*" (companies cannot commit crimes), because behind any criminal act in business there is always one or more individuals. Liszt was concerned with preventing executives who committed crimes from hiding behind their organizations.[10]

One of the few philosophers to directly apply philosophical principles to the corporate world is Adela Cortina, a Spanish academic who has made a major contribution to the study of business ethics and corporate responsibility.

After graduating in Philosophy and Literature at the University of Valencia in 1968, she entered the institution's department of Metaphysics, where she defended her doctoral thesis on God in Kantian philosophy. The early years of her thinking reflects the influence of critical theory, having spent part of her postdoctoral studies at the University of Munich. However, her later works, some in collaboration with other colleagues, including her husband and professor of Philosophy at Valencia University, Jesús Conill, show the influence of the neo-contractualism proposed by John Rawls and other Anglo-American academics such as Ronald Dworkin. It is worth noting that until the last quarter of the twentieth century most European university philosophy departments had a marked orientation toward German and French philosophy. The interest in Anglo-American philosophy is thanks to the efforts of a number of professionals who went against the mainstream.

Cortina became Professor of Moral Philosophy at the University of Valencia in 1986 and taught there until her retirement in 2017. During her career, she has written extensively for a wider public, contributing to leading Spanish newspapers such as *El País* or *Abc* on applied ethics, the challenges of immigration, war or bioethics. She is also a member of government advisory bodies such as the National Commission on Assisted Human Reproduction and the Advisory Committee on the Ethics of Scientific and Technological Research. Her 2017 book *Aporofobia*[11]—a term she invented by herself and refers to a fear of the poor—compares different types of phobias and proposes ways to overcome them.

Business Ethics: An Oxymoron?

I have long believed that an interdisciplinary approach to study, including business, favors innovation and provides new and productive research ideas. True innovation often lies at the nexus of different disciplines. Among the most recent opportunities in this regard are the combination of biology and philosophy, technology and law and business and psychology, which is why we should celebrate the decision of a philosopher originally oriented toward metaphysics to enter the field of business ethics.

Cortina explains how business and ethics have traditionally run in parallel. Indeed, most people still think that business decisions are amoral, that is, they are neither good nor bad from an ethical point of view. Instead, Cortina suggests practical and moral arguments for exploring the development of an ethics of business. Practical, because companies are subject to public opinion and the decisions their managers take are evaluated not only from a legal perspective, but a moral one also. In addition, business has lost much social legitimacy due to recent management scandals and the financial crisis of the last decade.

From a moral and ethical perspective, Cortina argues that companies, as social organizations, contribute to forming what she calls the civic ethics shared by the wider community.

Cortina's background in metaphysics comes to the fore in her first work on business ethics, where she states: "The goal of business activity is the *satisfaction of human needs* through the implementation of a capital, of which an essential part is human capital."[12] Establishing a definition that satisfies all stakeholders in a company is not easy, but I'm unsure if Cortina's would satisfy many business leaders. Meeting human needs is the goal of many other social institutions, including the state; while the chief reasons entrepreneurs set up companies include a desire to make money, break new ground, change the world or satisfy personal ambitions.

Taking a more constructivist approach, Cortina proposes that a company's ethics are rooted in the "quality of products and management, honesty in service, mutual respect in the internal and external relations of the company, the cooperation through which we jointly aspire to quality and solidarity, which consist in fully exploiting our abilities so that everybody can benefit from them, creativity, initiative, the spirit of risk."[13]

Cortina shares US academic and marketing expert Gene Brown's view on moral philosophy: Its purpose is not to make people better, but to make morally justifiable decisions. To provide a better framework for moral decision-making in business, Cortina uses Max Weber's distinction between the ethics of conviction and the ethics of responsibility, originally applied to politics and the arguments governments use to justify their actions.[14] The ethics of conviction argue that one must always act in accordance with some principle or norm, regardless of the results, a view that echoes deontological positions. But Weber doesn't believe politicians should behave like cosmic-ethical rationalists with no concern for the consequences of their decisions.

Furthermore, the ethics of conviction sometimes clash with what are known as antinomies of action: Good acts can result in bad outcomes and vice versa. Moral dilemmas present precisely these types of antinomies in situations such as supposedly just wars or assassinating tyrants, not to mention many other situations in daily life when we have to choose the lesser of two or more evils. There are many cases in management reflecting those dilemmas, such as downsizing a company or accepting the idea of being less profitable; choosing between short-term and long-term impact initiatives; or releasing full or partial information when the company is in crisis.

Some of these cases bring to mind a principle that is easy to say, but difficult to apply: *fiat iustitia et pereat mundus* (let justice be done and let the world perish). In business, this would mean apply ethical principles absolutely, even if it meant a company going under, the loss of jobs and other damages. But we know that on occasion, it is preferable to look for a compromise solution and avoid "letting the world perish", rather than accept the consequences of an action generating systemic or generalized damage. For example, when the federal reserve injected liquidity into the financial system in 2007 to avoid further damage, rather than letting the banks go under, even though we knew that many of them had indulged in unprofessional behavior.

Therefore, Weber argues, we need an ethic of responsibility to address the consequences of our actions and to what extent, under certain circumstances, questionable means can be used to try to achieve certain positive outcomes. The key lies in the balance between both types of ethics, convictions and responsibility.

Cortina relates this approach to K.O. Apel's theory of communicative rationality: in essence, cases where our convictions conflict with responsibility and the consequences of our actions.[15] The key is to be able to justify a decision using reasonable arguments that can be explained openly. The morally correct decision, according to this approach, is one can be argued in an open discussion and that most, if not all, people will understand. Warren Buffet's remark about what decisions made by managers are ethical serves as an example: Those that can be published in a newspaper the next day and do not question their leadership.[16]

From my experiences in management education, I can verify the validity of this approach. For example, when discussing business ethics in multicultural groups such as corruption or bribery, I have seen how the debate leads to a convergence of analyses and decisions, regardless of diversity, contradicting Aristotle's assertion that "fire burns both in Hellas and Persia, but ideas about good and evil change from one place to another."[17] From a moral perspective, conceptualizing ethical dilemmas, discussing them in public, for example, through the case method and dealing with specific assumptions, should lead to better decision-making.

The Rise of Corporate Social Responsibility

One of the phenomena resulting from the rise of business ethics and the professional ethics of the manager is corporate social responsibility (CSR). In short, CSR assumes that as social organizations, businesses must not only obey the law but also the basic principles that are part of the wider community's morals. At the same time, they should also assess their impact on society and the environment, as well as respecting the goal of sustainability. A manifestation of this phenomenon has been the triple bottom line, corporate reports that go beyond the annual audited financial statements to include a quantitative assessment of the company's impact on society and the environment. This exercise has become mandatory, for example, in member states of the European Union.

Initially, CSR was seen by its critics as little more than a PR exercise, and in fact in many companies CSR policies were coordinated by the corporate communication department. Over time, however, they have become increasingly relevant and in a growing number of organizations the CEO is directly involved in their development and promotion.

The conclusions of a 2015 study by Rangan, Chase and Karin on CSR practices, mainly in the United States, published in *The Harvard Business Review*[18] acknowledges that efforts have varied in their application and success. Furthermore, while policies must be justified in terms of their impact on the income statement, measuring the impact of CSR initiatives is difficult. The writers say the objectives of CSR fall into three main categories. In the first, the focus is on philanthropy, for example, by contributing to causes. In these cases, there is no attempt to obtain any benefit or synergy in return.

In a second category, are companies that invest in CSR practices to improve their operational effectiveness, for example, by implementing measures to prevent waste or emissions, thereby reducing their costs; or by investing to improve the working environment, health conditions and employees' education, resulting in greater motivation and improved performance.

A third category is that of transforming the business model and further developing the company, particularly to face the challenges of sustainability, while also improving economic performance. This third largely applies to the companies of the future, where their activities will be designed not only to fulfill, but to enhance their social commitment.

The important thing for the authors of this study is that each company's CSR practices and the mechanisms for measuring their success, as well as the evaluation of their economic impact, are consistent with their corporate strategy and supported by senior management.

Some academics question whether CSR practices necessarily have any positive impact on a company's performance. For example, a study published by the Conference Board, the New York-based business research group, concluded that the reasons that drive companies to enact ethics codes vary across cultures. Codes that are based on considerations of bottom-line success are much more popular in the United States. In fact, the study revealed that 64% of the ethical codes of US corporations are based on "instrumental" or utilitarian reasons, whereas 60% of the codes of European corporations are fueled by adherence to certain ethical values.[19] This data confirms that philosophical worldviews and business ethics are culturally based. Furthermore, researchers who compare US and European corporate cultures have emphasized that the former pivot on the principle of shareholder supremacy, while the latter are based on a wider conception of stakeholders, something that evidently shapes business ethics as well as corporate governance around the world.

Two arguments are typically used to justify adopting CSR practices and business ethics in general, which I call the business case and the moral case.

The *business case* justifies making ethical decisions in a company, such as implementing diversity and inclusion policies, that will improve economic performance. There are studies that show, for example, how companies whose boards reflect greater gender diversity on their boards or in senior management positions perform better. Similarly, the number of papers in journals showing the improved financial performance associated with implementing CSR initiatives has increased. Nevertheless, other reports show how some initiatives to promote diversity can have negative effects. As is often said about any initiative, 80% of success depends on implementation.

There is also evidence challenging the direct correlation between CSR and profitability: Fast-growing, profitable companies can afford to implement such policies. In short, are CSR programs the cause or the effect of profitability? For companies with financial problems, CSR is a luxury they cannot afford. Sumantra Ghoshal, as noted earlier, has criticized the use of the scientific cause-effect paradigm to explain a complex organizational phenomenon.

In an ideal world, the decision to implement CSR policies would be based on the moral case. Diversity programs, refusing to pay bribes or making sustainable products should be moral questions, matters of principle.

Following Weber, Cortina says arguments based on principle or conviction should not prevail where the consequences would be negative. There is a balance between both approaches that must be resolved through public debate. As with any other ethical issue, we find ourselves in a situation where the basic arguments underlying our decisions are internal and relate to our values and principles and that are more important than the results of our actions, even if not decisively.

Cortina turns to Nietzsche to explain why most entrepreneurs try to avoid morally unacceptable decisions: scandal, the loss of reputation. In *The Joyful Wisdom*, the German philosopher famously wrote that it is easier to cope with a bad conscience than a bad reputation. Cortina argues that while the fields of consciousness and reputation were traditionally separate, the former in the individual's inner world, the second in the outside world, the truth is that both are connected. This is because "the origin of moral conscience consists of the social instincts of human beings; this allows us to constitute a network of conditions that the non-human animal lacks, such as approval, reason, self-interest, instruction, habit and religious feelings."[20]

This argument seemingly bridges the chasm between the internal and external spheres seems. As Cortina adds, the truth is that shame and the desire for reputation have been decisive for the survival of the human race as well the individual: "Consciousness helps us make decisions to maintain our social reputation and to seem worthy people, because it is the means to reach self-esteem, bearing in mind that self-esteem is an asset nobody would want to give up."[21]

It seems that practical reasons, such as shame or the fear of losing our reputation, have become valid motives for dealing with moral dilemmas.

Business ethics is an area that has evolved considerably over the last thirty or forty years, with most business schools now covering it. Nevertheless, there is some skepticism about the usefulness of such initiatives. As noted earlier in this book, a recent event does, however, suggest we may have reached a turning point. In 2019, the Business Roundtable, which represents some 200 major US companies, among them JP Morgan, Amazon and General Motors, explicitly accepted a responsibility for shareholders, workers, suppliers and communities.[22] I remember that until relatively recently, when I used the term stakeholders at conferences in the United States, business people saw it as somehow "socialist" and more applicable to Europe. For most, Milton Friedman's maxim that the only responsibility of companies was to maximize shareholder value still held true.[23]

The Business Roundtable now believes that "companies should protect the environment and treat workers with dignity and respect, while also delivering long term profit for shareholders."[24] An important step, although perhaps, the best is yet to come.

Fear of the Poor

The globalization of contemporary society is, in my opinion, irreversible, for three main reasons: the impact of new technologies, the cosmopolitan profile of the millennial generation and the rise of entrepreneurship. Globalization has produced two conflicting effects. On the one hand, the extension of ideas, practices and homogeneous tastes. Young people socialize through social networks, eat pizza and share the ideal of sustainability regardless of the culture to which they belong.

Paradoxically, the other side of globalization is an increased emphasis on identity, which is sometimes magnified to differentiate individuals from other communities. This instinct, taken to its extreme, can exacerbate feelings that can damage coexistence: phobias toward other groups of people, usually minorities, as well as nationalism and xenophobia. There seems to be a growing rejection of anything or anyone deemed as different, so contrary to the spirit of tolerance essential to all true democracies: "The rejection of the other is legitimized. This is a key point in the world of group phobias: the conviction that there is an asymmetric relationship: race, ethnicity, sexual orientation, religious or atheist beliefs on the part of those who believe themselves superior toward those they make an object of rejection."[25]

There are many types of phobias: hatred of women, other races and religions are perhaps the most common. The business world is not exempt from this and although many studies show how diversity policies can drive innovation and improve the bottom line, there are still many organizations closed to change and to globalization.

Cortina addresses a specific type of phobia, aporophobia, a term she defines as an aversion to the poor, those seemingly unable to offer anything in exchange for what they receive. She explains how opposition to immigration from emerging countries such as we have seen in Europe from Africa the Middle East or in the United States toward its southern neighbors is in large part a rejection of the poor rather than one based on cultural, religious or racial differences, and she points to how incomers with skills and education are often much more welcome, as are those prepared to make large investments, regardless of where they come from.

At the same time, Cortina explains that aporophobia is a trait most of us share, and that in general we prefer abundance and wealth over scarcity and poverty: "All human beings are aporophobic, and this has its roots in our brains as well as how we construct society. It can and should be modified, if we take at least two of the keys of our culture: respect for the dignity of others and compassion, understood as the ability to perceive the suffering of others and to commit to prevent it."[26]

All phobias, Cortina explains, are related. She identifies five characteristics of hate speech: (i) It is directed against the individual for belonging to a particular group; (ii) that group is stigmatized by attributing to it acts seen as detrimental to society, for example, crime; (iii) the group is placed in the spotlight of discourse and policy and portrayed as enemies of the identity of society; (iv) those who harbor a phobia against others are convinced that there is a structural inequality with respect to other groups and feel a certain moral superiority over them; and finally (iv) they use inconsistent, false or fallacious arguments in their defense.[27]

This depiction of hate speech brings to mind not only episodes from the past, but can be found today in many democratically advanced countries. For the purpose of this work, I am particularly interested in exploring how to prevent these types of phobias from taking root in businesses.

As Cortina argues, the most effective instrument to cultivate respect for diversity and inclusion is through education. We need to develop training programs within companies to promote of diversity and inclusion. My experience and my conviction based on ample research and in my previous writing is that embracing diversity, cultivating a sense of belonging to humanity regardless of other people's religion, culture, ethnicity, gender, sexual orientation or class, helps develop emotional intelligence and in the process strengthens our openness to innovation and creativity and any other number of virtues, all of which can only facilitate personal relationships and professional success.

Takeaways

- Business and ethics are not separate worlds. As with other professions, the evolution of management has, over time, generated a professional deontology values and principles of a practical nature that serve as a reference in the face of dilemmas that offer a range of options.
- In line with Max Weber, we can approach moral dilemmas using one of two models: ethics based on conviction, using absolute principles; and the ethics of responsibility, which modulates principles in light of the likely outcome of a decision. The acid test here is whether we can publicly justify a decision, however controversial it might be.
- The evolution of business ethics, along with many of the ideas developed within CSR, is leading companies to communicate their sustainability standards more effectively and transparently, making them more accountable not just to shareholders, but to a wider group of stakeholders.
- We also need to use our critical faculties and get to know other cultures better so as to see hate speech for what it is: dangerous stereotypes based on ignorance of other groups.

Notes

1. All quotes in this section follow an interview between Inés Temple and the author on August 13, 2019.
2. S.J. Sucher and S. Gupta, Layoffs That Don't Break Your Company, *Harvard Business Review* (May–June 2018).
3. S. Iniguez de Onzono, *Cosmopolitan Managers: Executive Education That Works* (London: Palgrave Macmillan, 2016); Ch. 3.3.
4. I. Temple, *Usted, S.A.* (Lima: Editorial Planeta, 2015); Kindle ed.
5. Ibid., Kindle ed., loc. 209–210.
6. Ibid., Kindle ed., loc. 523.
7. D.R. Conant, What Losing My Job Taught Me About Leading, *Harvard Business Review* (March 18, 2013); C. Knoess, R. Harbour, and S. Scemama, Prepare Your Workforce for the Automation Age, *Harvard Business Review* (November 23, 2016).
8. I. Kant, *Groundwork for the Metaphysics of Morals*, Thomas E. Hill, Jr. and Arnulf Zweig (trans. and eds.) (Oxford and New York, NY: Oxford University Press, 2002); p. 199.
9. P. Drucker, Management's New Paradigms, *Forbes*, December 5, 1998.
10. V. Martínez Patón, *La doctrina societas delinquere non potest. Responsibilidad penal de ls personas jurídicas* (Buenos Aires: Editorial B de F, 2018).

11. A. Cortina, *Aporofobia, el rechazo al pobre. Un desafío para la democracia* (Barcelona: Planeta, 2017).
12. A. Cortina (ed.) *Etica de la Empresa. Claves para Una Nueva Cultura Empresarial* (Madrid: Trotta, 1994); p. 43.
13. Ibid.
14. *Max Weber*, in *Stanford Encyclopedia of Philosophy*, revised November 27, 2017. https://plato.stanford.edu/entries/weber/#EthConRes.
15. A. Cortina, D. García-Marzá, and J. Conill (eds.), *Public Reason and Applied Ethics: The Ways of Practical Reason in a Pluralist Society (Law, Ethics and Economics)* (Oxford and New York, NY: Routledge, 2008).
16. Known as Warren Buffett's rule of thumb: "I want employees to ask themselves whether they are willing to have any contemplatedact appear the next day on the front page of their local paper" (quoted in S. Iniguez de Onzono, *The Learning Curve: How Business Schools Are Reinventing Education* [London: Palgrave Macmillan, 2011]; p. 27).
17. Aristotle, *Nichomachean Ethics*, C.D.C Reeve (trans.) (Indianapolis: Hacket Publishing, 2014); p. 89.
18. V.K. Rangan, L. Chase, and S. Karim, The Truth About CSR, *Harvard Business Review* (January–February 2015).
19. The Conference Board, https://www.conference-board.org/blog/postdetail.cfm?post=6936.
20. A. Cortina, *Aporofobia, el rechazo al pobre: Un desafío para la democracia*, op. cit., Kindle ed., loc. 1308.
21. A. Cortina, *Aporofobia, el rechazo al pobre: Un desafío para la democracia*, op. cit., Kindle ed., loc. 1384.
22. R. Henderson and P. Temple-West, Group of US Corporate Leaders Ditches Shareholder-First Mantra: Business Roundtable Urges Companies to Consider the Environment and Workers as Well as the Pursuit of Profit, *Financial Times*, August 19, 2019.
23. M. Friedman, The Social Responsibility of Business Is to Increase Its Profits, *New York Times Magazine*, September 13, 1970.
24. R. Henderson and P. Temple-West, op. cit., ibid.
25. A. Cortina, *Aporofobia, el rechazo al pobre: Un desafío para la democracia*, op. cit., Kindle ed., loc. 140.
26. Ibid., Kindle ed., loc. 100.
27. Ibid.

11

Vision: Simone de Beauvoir/Usha Prashar

An Agent of Change: Baroness Usha Prashar[1]

On September 10, 2019, the day after British Prime Minister Boris Johnson had prorogued Parliament, I visited the House of Lords. My appointment was with the Right Honourable the Baroness Prashar of Runnymede, a crossbench member since 1999. The Palace of Westminster was quiet, with few people around.

I was met by the Baroness in the vestibule, from where we headed to the cafeteria, a mix of traditional English pub and Gentleman's club with views across the Thames. The room is dominated by a vast painting of the Battle of Cape Saint Vincent, when a British naval contingent defeated a much larger Spanish fleet on Saint Valentine's day, 1797, during the French Revolutionary Wars. Due to the prorogation, no food was available, but we were at least able to find a cup of coffee.

Prashar is an engaging woman: charismatic, approachable and with an encyclopedic knowledge. We immediately struck up a conversation during which she revealed her outstanding capacity to call up facts, dates and people, along with the intelligent virtue of explaining complex ideas in context. She is nothing if not cosmopolitan: Born in Kenya of Indian parentage, she has lived most of her life in Britain. She combines the cultures of three continents, their visions and different customs. This syncretism has allowed her to analyze complex issues from different perspectives over the course of her career.

She remembers her childhood in Nairobi and the rigid racial strata of the British colonial system: "In pre-independence Kenya, there was a real demarcation between the Asians, the Africans and the Europeans. I do remember ours was the only dining table where my father invited his African friends to sit with us. This was unusual, because the deal then was that the British ruled, the Asians were the traders, and Africans basically provided services. I observed discrimination and I saw how my father reacted to it."

Her opportunity to move to Britain came about because, as an Asian, she could not study in Kenya: "There were separate schools for Asians, Africans and Europeans. If you wanted to take A levels, there were no facilities. I applied to go to an English school, this was on the cusp of independence. I wasn't admitted because I was not white. Ironically, I got an admission to come and do my A levels in Yorkshire, in the north of England. I was the school's first overseas student."

During her time at high school, Prashar remembers that having to answer questions about where she came from to fellow students and her teachers allowed her to develop a narrative about Indian culture and her cross-cultural experiences. At the same time, she would accompany her sister-in-law, a health visitor, to translate for Pakistani immigrants, which gave her a keen understanding of discrimination, creating an interest in social policy.

She studied sociology at Leeds University. It was her intention to go back to Kenya, but the political situation changed both in Kenya and in the UK with the advent of 1968 Immigration Act. In the circumstances, she decided to attend University of Glasgow for post-graduate qualifications.

> In this country there was a tradition that if you wanted to institute a new policy, you did it in Scotland, as a trial, to see how it worked. And at that time, they had published the Kilbrandon report, which was about how you organize social administration. So, I decided to do social administration at Glasgow University. When I looked at the course it was basically about training one to be a social worker which did not appeal to me. I did not want to be a social worker. I wanted to be an agent of change. I believe in social action.

Since finishing university, Prashar's career has been impactful, committed and fascinating. She has been a pioneer in leading fourth-sector organizations, contributing decisively to professionalizing non-governmental bodies. She's been asked many times over the years if she sees herself more as a thinker or a doer and describes herself as "a thinker who does."

Prashar's first job was as an assistant conciliation officer for the then Race Relations Board, set up in the wake of the Race Relations Act of 1968. Race was being used as an issue by some politicians, notably Enoch Powell, who had delivered his infamous "Rivers of Blood" speech earlier that year, predicting race riots in Britain as a result of immigration and that cost him his political career.

Her work preparing civil action suits gave Prashar a deeper understanding of the nature of discrimination, the importance of dialogue and listening to the views and fears of others, and of how government works. Her efforts helped toward dismantling the system of bussing children from Pakistani, Indian and Caribbean families in the north of England to schools sometimes up to an hour away from where they lived as part of a quota policy that limited immigrant numbers in schools to 30%.

She was then headhunted by the Runnymede Trust, the influential race equality think tank, which after a year, in 1977, she then ran for 7 years. The organization's philosophy was to develop evidence-based research that could be used in government policy.

The Runnymede Trust was responsible for understanding how so-called indirect discrimination works through policies like bussing. It also brought to the public's attention the issue of institutionalized racism, particularly in the wake of the riots in Brixton, London, in 1981, which were the subject of a report overseen by Lord Scarman, which pointed to the excessive use of force used by the Metropolitan Police against the Afro-Caribbean community resident in the area.

Scarman was careful not to accuse the police of institutionalized racism in his report, instead pointing to the actions of individuals within the capital's police force. Prashar responded with an article in the influential Sunday newspaper The Observer criticizing the report for its failings in this regard.

Prashar also organized several effective initiatives from Runnymede, such as bringing together US and British judges to share their views and experiences on discrimination, along with a report on media coverage of conflicts with African immigrants carried out with Peter Evans of The Times. This approach foreshadowed later studies on the media's narratives of conflict in society, particularly in relation to immigration, an issue that has become more prescient with the emergence of the social networks.

Her experiences led Prashar to better understand the many ways in which discrimination works: "It's like litmus paper, it tells you what's wrong with your organization as a whole," which led her to become involved in more mainstream challenges to do with wider issues, as a result of which she joined the Policy Studies Institute, looking at primary health care.

She then went on to work with the National Council for Voluntary Organizations (NCVO), the body that brings together NGOS, voluntary associations and community service groups. She was the first woman and a minority person to hold this post. This was in 1984.

This transition from race related organizations to "a mainstream" organization sent strong message. I got lot of letters and messages from women and minorities saying: "Gosh, if you have done it, we can do it too."

She is still Honorary President of Community Foundations. Prashar quotes Lord Beveridge on the importance of the sector: "Voluntary action is the mark of a free society," adding, "freedom of association has been the lifeblood of the UK voluntary activity." As if to illustrate this, while I am interviewing Prashar, Danny Sriskandarajah, CEO of OXFAM, who is visiting the House, approaches our table and greets her. She then continues:

> Compared to anywhere in Europe, voluntary activity in the UK has been really up there. This experience brought two things home for me: one, it provided me with an opportunity to not only look at organizational change, but also the importance of social movements to bring about change.
>
> …Now, turning to management style, the NCVO had been through a little bit of a difficult period. Its director left, they appointed someone who didn't turn out to be right. So, when I joined, the organization was in a little bit of disarray, it had a deficit, it was rudderless, and it wasn't acting, in my view, as a proper membership organization. Some of the latter member charities had left because they thought it was not acting as a membership body and instead trying to compete with its members.
>
> So, I was asking myself, how can I change all this? Apart from dealing with a quarter of a million-pound deficit – you can imagine in 1984, it was a lot of money – I set about re-organizing it to give it a clear direction, looking at two aspects: one was the policy side; the other was local action. And, at that time, rural community councils were part of the NCVO, as was the voluntary action community; they wanted independence, which they were given. I then focused on building a real membership organization and streamlining its processes.

Prashar took advantage of the challenge to develop her own approach to tackling the strategic threats to the organization based on her own leadership style, which she had developed over the years. "My style was very consultative: I talked to people, I built alliances.

> My approach in every organization has been to understand what's the problem you're trying to solve, and once you've analyzed that, then you've got to know where you want to be, and then, how you get there. And, within that, to me there are some essential values: involvement, engaging and working with people. My philosophy is, if you do things for the right reason you succeed.

When you're the leader, never try to score all your own goals, instead, empower other people to score the goals, this way you motivate other people. At the same time, the challenges facing us in the external world were enormous: it was the era of Mrs. Thatcher, the focus was on curtailing campaigning by voluntary organisations. She saw them purely as delivering services to people. In other words, quietly: just get on and deliver, do not agitate. NCVO succeeded in protecting the right of voluntary organizations to campaign."

In Prashar's opinion, there are two types of manager: "coasters, who coast along in a job, and sprinters, who have a challenge, deal with it and then move on." She sees herself as a sprinter. After transforming the NCVO, she served as a member of the Royal Commission on Criminal Justice, along with the Lord Chancellor's Advisory Committee on Legal Education and Conduct. She also took on the position of non-executive director at Channel 4, later doing the same at ITV. She was also appointed to a range of roles in several international institutions.

She has fond memories of her next position, as Executive Chairman of the Parole Board of England and Wales, the first woman to hold the post. As with her previous jobs, she set about improving things in an organization that was failing prisoners, as well as society.

> When I got there, it was worse than Kafka. I'm not exaggerating, there were piles of files everywhere, mainly of complaints from MPs on behalf of their constituents who were in prison waiting to hear about their parole. It turned out that only 27% of people heard their decisions on time. They were languishing in prison, as a result, they were complaining to their MPs. MPs were writing to the Parole Board, the Parole Board had to investigate why there was a delay? This meant, the staff were spending their time responding to the complaints and the casework didn't get done.

Again, she applied her modus operandi of identifying the problem and then applying the solution. The key link in the system was the parole clerks at prisons, who did not have the status to get the process moving. By highlighting their role and encouraging them to be more involved in finding a solution and engaging all the others who were crucial to the process she managed to get the decision-making process working. By the time she left, 94% of the paroles heard their decisions on time.

Prashar was made a peer in 1999, joining the House of Lords, since when she has continued to take on a growing number of challenges. Some of these include: First Civil Services Commissioner, inaugural Chairman of the Judicial Appointments Commission, Chairman and then President of the Royal Commonwealth Society, Member of the Iraq Inquiry and Deputy Chair of the British Council, which is when I first met her, as well as the honor of working with her as member of IE Business School's International Advisory Board.

When I asked her how she felt being the only woman presiding over or sitting on boards and committees, she replied:

> In all honesty, I took always took the view that I am not going to be conscious I am a woman or a minority. To me, I'm a person. I am clear about what I have to offer. Self-awareness and confidence are quite important as is self-esteem. I never approached any job I did being conscious that I am a minority or a woman. That did not inhibit me in any way. I just did the job and was very focused on what I had to do.

After my meeting with Prashar at Westminster Palace, I went to Heathrow to catch my flight back to Madrid. A British Airways pilots' strike had left the airport empty, a strange and unsettling sight. The UK seemed closed that day. But anglophile that I am, I could only hope that the country I consider my second home would emerge from its predicaments as soon as possible. There is certainly a need for more Prashar in this world.

Simone de Beauvoir: The Beginnings of Feminist Philosophy

When discussing the factors that have contributed most to changing the business landscape in recent years, globalization, technology, sustainability and environment awareness are usually cited.[2] However, there is an additional element that has already made a significant impact in recent decades and that will influence the future of interpersonal relationships: feminism, which is helping drive diversity and inclusion.[3]

Even so, there are still many people who are suspicious or even hostile toward the idea of feminism, in many cases because of their ignorance of its fundamental arguments. But if the essence of feminism is the recognition and implementation of equal rights for men and women, who would not subscribe to such a proposition? Yet asked if they consider themselves feminists, many men—and a good number of women—would probably say no, perhaps without realizing that what they are really saying is that they do not believe in human rights.

To further complicate matters, there are a wide range of views as to how the project of implementing equal rights should be carried out in our societies and in business. There are many different points of view, as in other areas of practical reasoning, and of course different and sometimes conflicting currents within feminism itself. We can see feminism as a *concept*, that of equality between men and women, but there are many differing *conceptions* about its meaning and application. My intention here is not to dilute the importance or urgency of the feminist task, but rather to explain feminism in context to avoid dogmatic positions and to convince readers of its vital role in our societies.

Given that this book's focus is on philosophy, we might usefully start with Simone de Beauvoir, who is widely recognized as one of the founders of modern feminism. Published in 1949, her book *The Second Sex*[4] immediately generated widespread controversy. From a purely philosophical point of view, it was both innovative and a major contribution to the existentialist canon.

Beauvoir poses the question "What is a woman?". But she is not concerned with biology, anthropology or even psychology, but instead with philosophy. What's more, as she points out, no philosopher had ever asked the question: until then, philosophy had at best been concerned with "human beings" or more frequently "man" as a singular entity supposedly encompassing both sexes.

As Beauvoir notes, most classical philosophers were hostile toward women. Pythagoras wrote: "There is a good principle that created order, light and man, and a bad principle that created chaos, darkness and woman." Aristotle believed: "Female is female by virtue of a certain lack of qualities," noting: "We have to consider the character of woman as naturally flawed." St. Thomas Aquinas described women as "defective and misbegotten." Beauvoir reviews references to women in the Bible and literature down the centuries, where at best they exist in terms of their complementarity or their alterity to men, finally asking: "Why don't women question male sovereignty?"[5]

The basic argument of her book might be summarized by her assertion that "a woman is not born, but instead becomes one." What defines how women are and how they behave throughout their lives, is not their sex, but the role society assigns to them: "And yet we are told that femininity is in danger; we are exhorted to be women, remain women, become women. It would appear, then, that every female human being is not necessarily a woman; to be so considered she must share in that mysterious and threatened reality known as femininity."[6]

In contrast to the archetype of the married woman, whose life is limited to the home and raising children, Beauvoir insisted that women could and should choose from any number of options and opportunities. In the 70 years since the publication of *The Second Sex*, women have succeeded in opening new avenues for professional and personal achievement, and today it sounds absurd to speak of a profile or archetypal ideal woman, of an essence of what a woman is or should be. There is still much to do, but there are now innumerable roles and functions women can choose from and more will doubtless come. As Beauvoir notes: "But conceptualism has lost ground. The biological and social sciences no longer admit the existence of unchangeably fixed entities that determine given characteristics, such as those ascribed to woman, the Jew, or the Negro. Science regards any characteristic as a reaction dependent in part upon a situation."[7]

The feminism Beauvoir proposes is close to the existentialist philosophy propositioned by Jean-Paul Sartre: "existence precedes essence."[8] In other words, we are what we live, we are the sum of our experiences, our circumstances, and not what a concept or previous idea determines. This is the fundamental thesis of Beauvoir, who distinguishes between the biological fact of sex and the cultural construction of gender, which is formed by conventions, attitudes, behaviors and clichés that society usually associates with either sex. For Beauvoir, there are no biological elements that determine the conventions that relate to be a woman. As we know, this key distinction between sex and gender has been of enormous use beyond feminism in the debate on sexual orientation and identity and queer theory.

Beauvoir's own life was exceptional.[9] She was born into a Parisian bourgeois family, although the collapse of her maternal grandfather's bank caused some economic hardship and social stigma. Her father, now financially dependent on his wife and no longer able to provide a dowry for his daughter, saw that the best way forward for his intelligent daughter was study. As a result, Beauvoir becomes one of the first women to graduate from the Sorbonne, going on to attend the Ecole Normale Superieure, where she would obtain second place in the *agrégation*, France's national exam that ranks every student and typical of the supposed meritocracy of French educational institutions. First place went to Sartre, who would be her companion for the rest of her life.

In the opinion of some historians of philosophy, Beauvoir has not been given the recognition she deserves. This is for two main reasons: Firstly because she was overshadowed by Sartre, although US academic William McBride has argued that *The Second Sex* is in many ways "both more original than Sartre's writing and more evocative of the spirit of its age."[10]

The second reason Beauvoir has been sidelined as a philosopher is because she chose to write specifically about women: Only in recent years, thanks to the work of other feminist writers, along with protest movements such as #ME TOO,[11] has her thinking found broader recognition among a new generation of feminists.

In addition, as with other female philosophers in this book, Beauvoir explored other areas of writing. She was a successful novelist: *The Mandarins*,[12] which won the prestigious Prix Goncourt Prize in 1954, is a portrait of post-war intellectual life in Paris, with veiled references to Sartre, Albert Camus and others. *Old Age*,[13] published in 1972, is an perceptive study into how age transforms our way of seeing the world, our thinking and feeling, and is on a par with the insights of Cicero, Seneca or Montaigne.

Nevertheless, *The Second Sex* remains Beauvoir's most important intellectual legacy. Marxist thinker Stella Sandford writes: "Deeply embedded in the European traditions of philosophy, especially phenomenology and existentialism, *The Second Sex* rests on two connected, specifically feminist, philosophical innovations: first, the gendering of phenomenological experience, and second, the positing of a novel question (albeit in a classical philosophical form) for existential ontology: What is a woman?" She adds that Beauvoir's work is also framed within critical theory, usually associated with the Frankfurt school and authors such as Theodor Adorno or Max Horkheimer, describing it as "a critique of the society that produces woman as Other. It presents 'woman' as she 'is interpreted in the existing order,' as what society actually makes of her precisely in order to question this state of affairs."[14]

Some 70 years after its publication, *The Second Sex* is still in print and widely read; in my opinion, it should be suggested reading for all undergraduates. And how can it help us in the daily practice of management?

To begin with, diversity and inclusion policies should be a priority in all companies: As I've explained, the case is both business and ethical. Over the course of my academic career, as a teacher and manager, my experience has been and remains that the debate on diversity in business remains woefully inadequate. In most advanced countries, with the exception of Scandinavia, women are still underrepresented in senior management, on boards and even MBA programs.[15] In addition, issues such as the wage gap and the lack of specific programs to help women integrate, along with the absence of a permanent discourse within business, suggests that change will only come through a combination of legislation and social activism. At the same time, we know that companies rarely self-regulate on issues other than short-term economic gains. If we leave the implementation of all diversity-related issues to organic development, it will be several decades before any kind of equitable landscape emerges, if at all.

For these reasons, I have always believed in affirmative action to speed up gender equality and diversity in business. I know that many people in business, including some female CEOs with whom I have discussed the subject, dismiss affirmative action as an imposition; I usually counter their objections by pointing out the huge progress made by the equality policies and mandatory quotas adopted in Scandinavia over the last 40 years. These may have been opposed initially, but they have managed to establish the most balanced integration and inclusion models on the planet. Little wonder that there have been more female than male prime ministers in these countries over the past years, that the boards of directors and senior management are balanced and that women are more equally represented in a range of sectors, including education.

I believe that educational institutions provide the most powerful platform to transfer the values that inform diversity and inclusion to students and tomorrow's leaders. Furthermore, in my experience, millennials and younger generations tend to be more sensitive toward these issues. That said, business schools and universities still have much to do to achieve better balances in the composition of student bodies and faculty, particularly when assigning tenure to academics.

Allow me to share the experience of IE Business School over the last two decades, where we have pursued an equality policy when hiring new faculty members. Currently, 44% of the full-time faculty is made up of women, which is at least ten percentage points higher than the average in our business school cluster.[16] This is no small achievement considering that doctoral programs in management are still mostly filled by men. An important outcome of a gender-balanced faculty—there is still room for improvement, and we are working in that direction—is that our students have female teachers that provide inspiration and with whom they may feel greater affinity, in addition to many other advantages. As recently as two years ago, I received an email from a graduate attending a joint program between a European and a US school, complaining that there hadn't been a single female teacher on her MBA.

I have looked at ways to boost diversity within business in *The Learning Curve*,[17] and here I would like to make a more focused, more specific recommendation I think could benefit organizations: supporting young female managers in the early stages of their professional development. A study by Bain & Company, shows that 43% of women at the beginning of their careers aspire to reach senior management positions, compared with 34% of men, but this percentage drops dramatically to 16% within just two years, while for men the figure is maintained. The study concludes that the reason is a lack of support from managers and supervisors, along with a lack of role models: "The majority of leaders celebrated in a corporate newsletter or an offsite meeting tend to consist of men hailed for pulling all-nighters or for networking their way through the golf course to land the big account." At the same time, for many women, these early stages of professional development coincide with starting a family. We have seen that in many advanced countries, women put off marriage and having children until they feel more secure in their careers.[18]

If companies implemented specific programs to guarantee the development of young female executives in those all-important early years, they would soon have much more diverse cadres. I believe business schools can also contribute to diversity in the following specific ways. First, as we have seen, by employing more female teachers to inspire and encourage our female students. Second, by promoting more research on diversity and inclusion issues, including the development of business feminism studies. Third, by working closely with companies to help their young female managers through coaching and mentorship programs. Fourth, by developing specific courses aimed at female students to strengthen their skills and abilities.

This last suggestion is the result of a meeting held with a group of female alumni from different schools two years ago, where I was told that on MBA programs, where the majority of students are still men, a "boys club" dynamic often developed in the classroom. Courses aimed specifically at women would help develop certain key skills such as leadership and negotiation suited to them by taking place in a more friendly environment.

Also, encouraging the creation of a culture that respects and embraces diversity and inclusion by teaching the principles of feminism will eventually change our approach to business, resulting in fairer and more sustainable companies.

Engagement and Speaking Out

As we are seeing in this chapter, one of the most frequent syndromes in human thought is the association of patterns or clichés that enable us to classify reality, map our surroundings and comprehend things in ways that allow us to take decisions and act. If someone declares themselves a feminist, we tend to assume they will be left-wing, an atheist or agnostic and support abortion rights, for example. Obviously, this association of preferences does not always respond to reality. Another example is the association that many people make between existentialism, a negative worldview, a depressive temperament and passivity. It is to be expected that some people will interpret *La Nausea* and other works by Sartre as nihilist, and furthermore, as many issues are difficult to explain, such as death, that we might as well disengage from the world, isolating ourselves from the outside and avoiding, as far as possible, events from impacting on us directly.

However, nothing could be further from the life-affirming attitude that characterized Beauvoir and Sartre's lives. They may have been stereotyped as spending their days at Café de Flore, in the Latin Quarter, chatting about insubstantial philosophical issues and commenting on the news, but the reality is that they took sides and were active in many causes of a social and political nature. In fact, their activism gave rise to the use of the idea of engaging with the world, now widely used, even in business, and that comes from the French verb *engager*, used to denote a commitment to ideas, taking sides, and trying to change things, regardless of the consequences. In the case of Beauvoir, her commitment to feminism is evident, and she disseminated her ideas not only through her work, but in her lectures, interviews, meetings and in the magazine *Les temps Modernes*, which she co-founded with Sartre. She met a remarkable number of personalities, not just intellectuals, but also politicians, among them Fidel Castro, Mao Zedong and Che Guevara.

Do We Grow Old, or Start a Second Life?

When Beauvoir published *Coming of Age* in 1970, at the age of 62, the average life expectancy in France was 65. Very few people had private pension plans, care homes were a rarity, and the elderly suffering from Alzheimer's disease or dementia was sometimes placed in psychiatric clinics alongside patients suffering from severe mental disorders.

Beauvoir initially seems to be addressing the issue of old age from a similar perspective to previous thinkers. Montaigne, for example, explained that growing older is a "privilege" and a "great favor." The sixteenth-century French philosopher, who wrote in his diaries how he was on the verge of death on one occasion, encouraged his readers by telling them: "Death is only a few bad moments at the end of life," adding: "If you don't know how to die, don't worry; Nature will tell you what to do on the spot, fully and adequately. She will do this job perfectly for you; don't bother your head about it."[19]

Writing almost 1500 years before, in Rome, Seneca, who was Nero's tutor until the emperor obliged him to commit suicide, argued that life offered meaning to us in all stages, especially old age, and that we retained the capacity to increase our understanding of the world around us, even if we might choose not to. As a Stoic, he believed in a certain detachment from material things and in strength of spirit: If you feel depressed or bored after retirement, just look around and be astonished by the varied and sublime nature of our world. According to Seneca, great comfort can be found in the contemplation of nature.[20] Beyond contemplation, it is also necessary to continue acquiring knowledge and to give meaning to one's life: "If you fail to grasp life, it will elude you. If you do grasp it, it will elude you anyway. So you must follow it - and 'you must drink quickly as though from a rapid stream that will not always flow'."[21]

Cicero, who predated Seneca by a century, was also optimistic about old age, arguing that we compensate for the decline of our physical faculties with the experience and intelligence we acquire over the years. He uses the analogy of the captain of a ship, generally older than his crew, who is respected for his knowledge, despite no longer being able to shin up the mast like the cabin boy.

While respecting the view that old age has much to offer, Beauvoir offers the until-then unique technique of examining old age through the prism of feminism. *Coming of Age* was written as a counterpart to *The Second Sex*[22] and has a similar structure. She explains that while old age is period of biological decline, this should not necessarily entail a feeling of oppression. Instead, it is the meaning society attributes to the final stages of life that makes it oppressive. As with women, the elderly in western societies are "the others." Beauvoir explains that in some civilizations elders are treated with an almost reverential respect and are regarded as interlocutors with the gods, the depositaries of the legacy of ancient generations. In East Asian countries such as China and Japan, this respect is reflected in social activities, treatment and initiatives for their care.

But in capitalist societies—and this is where Beauvoir's Marxist perspective also comes into play—where change is rapid, experience loses its value and those without an occupation that generates a return on capital quickly lose their social identity. She adds that retirement rarely provides opportunities to develop a personal identity. Instead, during retirement, we find ourselves "losing one's place in society, losing one's dignity and almost one's existence [*sa réalité*]."[23] She concludes that our treatment of the aged "exposes the failure of our entire civilization."[24]

Today, almost half a century after the publication of *Coming of Age*, conditions for the elderly have improved markedly in developed countries. Average life expectancy in France and western Europe is now around 82, while estimates suggest that advances in medicine, technology and biology mean that with each calendar year we gain three more months of life.

But while we in the developed world are living longer, thus delaying retirement age, I would identify three major issues relating to the senior members of society that have yet to be resolved.

Firstly, we need to reinvent the idea of retirement and redesign the system of financial assistance for the elderly to provide a decent and enjoyable life. Our pension systems and calculation of retirement ages were designed when life expectancy was nearly 20 years shorter than today and experts agree they are unsustainable. As I have proposed in *Cosmopolitan Managers*, one solution would be to create part-time, flexible jobs for the over-65s that draw on their particular skills, combined with training programs to adapt to new technology. This is an area where the private sector could play a role, rather than leaving such initiatives to governments. One of the characteristics I most admire about businesses in China and Japan is the respect there for retired workers, who are sometimes appointed a vice president or head of department, as well as being provided with resources for their care.

Another challenge for companies is integrating different generations and developing synergies that combine their respective talent. Within a few years, extending the retirement age will mean there can be as many as five or more generations within the same company, posing either a threat or an opportunity for senior management. Again, the best way to meet this challenge is through in-company training and education. This would help older employees recover the loss of personal identity that Beauvoir identified, and with it greater respect. More and more companies are now initiating reverse mentorship programs where younger employees advise their older colleagues in areas such as digital skills, technology management or social networks, as well as indicating new ways of learning and understanding the changing environment around them.

The third challenge is that of creating a culture of inclusion where the styles, ideas, fashions or perspective of seniors are regarded as part of the cultural mainstream. Specifically, this would mean seeing older people in advertisements, movies and television, novels and other areas of popular culture, rather than being associated solely with retirement or ill health. In any event, I believe changing demographics in developed countries will lead to this integration happening naturally and will not require extraordinary measures. In short, companies will necessarily have to adapt their products and services to the demands of an aging population.

Thanks to the feminist movement, driven by philosophers such as Beauvoir, the inequalities between men and women, in society and at work, have to a large extent been mitigated, although much remains to be done. As with feminism, perhaps we'll see a movement emerge in the coming years to fight for the full integration of the elderly, led by a new generation of senior writers such as Beauvoir, Cicero, Montaigne or Seneca.

Takeaways

Simone de Beauvoir is the keystone of feminist philosophy, a fascinating and necessary branch of the study. Exploration of women and their particular circumstances has been omitted or underplayed in traditional philosophy.

- Beauvoir argued that women are not so much born, as made. The role of culture, gender roles, the law and treatment by the state and institutions are the determining factors, creating normative conclusions based on highly questionable assumptions. Feminist philosophy's contribution has been hugely useful in helping us better understand the assumptions and concepts at the heart of our understanding of society, but that can be changed.
- Initiatives to drive diversity and inclusion may promote innovation and, if properly implemented and managed, result in higher returns.
- By analyzing gender discrimination, sexual orientation, identity and life choices, we can better address other problems related to social integration, such as our older population.

Notes

1. All quotes in this section are taken from an interview with Baroness Usha Prashar, London, 10 September 2019.
2. Vid. S. Iniguez de Onzono, *Cosmopolitan Managers: Executive Development That Works* (London: Palgrave Macmillan, 2016); Ch. 1.
3. Ibid., Ch. 7.

4. S. de Beauvoir, *The Second Sex* (New York: Barnes & Noble-Spark Publishing, 2003); references here are made to the Spanish edition: *El segundo sexo*, T. López Pardina (prologue), Alicia Marrorell (trans.) (Madrid: Cátedra, 2017); Kindle ed.
5. Ibid., position 990.
6. Ibid., position 430.
7. Ibid., posición 915.
8. J.P. Sartre, *Existentialism Is a Humanism*, C. Macomber (trans.) (New Haven: Yale University Press, 2007), p. vii.
9. Most biographical pieces on Beauvoir are taken from different articles in L. Hengehold and N. Bauer (eds.), *A Companion to Simone de Beauvoir* (Hoboken, NJ and Chichester, UK: Wiley, 2017).
10. W. McBride, *Sartre e Beauvoir all'asse del ventesimo secolo*; in P. Invitto, *La fenomenologiua e l'oltre-fenomenologia: Prendendo spunto dal pensiero francese* (Milan: Mimesis Edizioni), p. 95.
11. In my opinion, the best updates from the #Me Too Moment are published by *New York Times* gender editor, Jessica Bennett at: https://www.nytimes.com/series/metoo-moment.
12. S. de Beauvoir, *The Mandarins* (London: HarperCollins, 2005).
13. *La Viellesse* was translated initially as *Coming of Age*, Patrick O'Brian (trans.) (New York: W. W. Norton, 1972).
14. L. Hengehold and N. Bauer (eds.), *A Companion to Simone de Beauvoir*, op. cit., position 1563.
15. Data on the percentage of women on MBA programs may be found at the *Financial Times* MBA Rankings: http://rankings.ft.com/businessschoolrankings/global-mba-ranking-2019.
16. Ibid. Data related to top ranked business schools in 2019.
17. S. Iniguez de Onzono, *The Learning Curve: How Business Schools Are Reinventing Higher Education* (London: Palgrave Macmillan, 2011).
18. O. Badiesh and J. Coffman, Companies Drain Women's Ambition After Only 2 Years, *Harvard Business Review*, May 18, 2015.
19. S. Bakewell, *How to Live: Or a Life of Montaigne in One Question and Twenty Attempts at an Answer* (London: Random House, 2010); Kindle ed., p. 340.
20. Ibid., p. 544.
21. L.A. Seneca, *Letters from a Stoic* (London: Penguin, 1969); Letter 78.
22. S. Blackwell, op. cit., p. 799.
23. S. Kruks, *Beauvoir and the Marxist Question*; Chapter 19 in L. Hengehold and N. Bauer, op. cit., p. 235 (Kindle 8214).
24. Ibid., p. 244 (Kindle 8460).

12

Resolve: African Challenges/Ifeoma Idigbe

Women Hold the Keys to Africa's Future

I arrived in Lagos, Nigeria's commercial capital, in the early evening, and by now it was dark. A good friend had warned me about Nigerians' abrupt manners, their boisterousness and seemingly aggressive tone of voice. And once again, I discovered how wrong cultural stereotypes so often are. The people I met during my stay were polite, courteous and good-humored.

The journey from the airport to my hotel on Victoria Island was slow, and the traffic made it even slower as we crawled along wide avenues, over spectacular bridges and sometimes through the narrow streets of this frenetic and chaotic metropolis, the second largest in Africa, after Cairo. The layout is ad hoc and much of the city's infrastructure is badly maintained, like many other places I have visited in India or Brazil. There are people everywhere, from street sellers weaving in among the traffic, people chatting in groups on corners, to families gathered in parks and squares. Poverty and homelessness is evident, but like so many other cities in the developing world, the climate is a mitigating factor.

Lagos is a hive of human and commercial activity, bubbling over with the energy of a city that grows by the day. A showcase for the energy that characterizes a continent with the youngest population on the planet and the greatest economic growth potential, albeit tempered by any number of risks and threats.

It's easy to highlight Lagos' faults, but that is to miss the point: this is one of Africa's major business hubs, with a thriving and dynamic entrepreneurial scene. The pessimistic outlook shared by some analysts regarding the continent's outlook is distorted, in my opinion. Most headlines in the European press about Africa are negative, of the glass half-empty variety, constantly reporting epidemics, corruption, political crises, and do not reflect the continent's promising future and huge potential.

Similarly, positive narratives can be paternalistic, focusing on development issues, rather than highlighting the disruptive initiatives and real and potential opportunities for business. Africa, particularly the region south of the Sahara, has suffered from poor marketing, and what is needed is a narrative told by Africans themselves, one that highlights its history, the wealth of its Humanities, its culture, its artistic and literary expression. The world also needs to know the stories of the growing numbers of African entrepreneurs and their successes. We need African Jack Mases and Sheryl Sandbergs.

Africa's philosophical renaissance started when the continent began emerging from colonialism in the mid-1960s and universities began attracting a new generation of thinkers. The field has enjoyed significant growth in recent years, reflected in *A Companion to African Philosophy*,[1] edited in 2004 by Kwasi Wiredu, a Ghanaian who teaches at the University of South Florida. The book features more than 40 specially commissioned essays, ranging across disciplines and the ages.

Wiredu believes that African philosophy is currently in search of its identity, after centuries of colonialism that systematically imposed denial of all things African. This was compounded by the missionary movement, which also sought to eliminate African the culture and beliefs that lie at the heart of philosophical speculation, says Wiredu: "if an African idea proved to be irreducibly incompatible with a Christian one, it was due for correction in the interests of salvation."[2] Furthermore, accounts of the continent's philosophy as a whole have done the same, not realizing Africa's wide diversity in terms of peoples and ethnic groups, and consequently visions of the World.

Finally, most African philosophical ideas and models belong to the oral tradition, which has limited their survival and dissemination: "African philosophy was becoming hard to distinguish from a sort of informal anthropology," says Wiredu.[3]

Wiredu's book includes a piece by Nkiru Nzegwu, who teaches at Binghamton University, in New York, about feminist philosophy in Africa. In her opinion, intellectual approaches to gender by non-African writers have also been biased by their cultural conceptions, ignoring the idiosyncrasies and culture of the continent: "They reflect as well the binary opposition underlying Western epistemology in which women are defined in opposition to men, that is, are assigned converse attributes."[4] She applies a number of examples to back up her assertion, such as the meaning of woman in Igbo, the largest ethnic group in southeast Nigeria, Cameroon and Equatorial Guinea, which she says has different gender and femininity connotations to those in western societies: "nwanyi has most regularly been treated as synonymous with 'woman', even though they do not share the same attributes or conceptual scope. For instance, stance, nwanyi does not exclusively refer to an adult female person; it refers to both children and adults. It does not imply that females are psychologically passive beings who are or ought to be submissive and subordinate to men."[5]

This is a clear case of diversity, also in customs. The rescue and rehabilitation of African cultures and philosophies is gaining momentum, and we perhaps have something to learn from some of the ideas related to a more equitable and balanced society.

One of these ideas, which has always aroused my admiration, is the concept of *ubuntu*, found in the Zulu and Xhosa cultures of southern Africa. Ubuntu philosophy was behind the reconstruction and reconciliation sought by Nelson Mandela after he became president of South Africa in 1990 after 27 years in prison, facilitating a peaceful political transition. Its meaning can be synthesized as "a person becomes human through other people."[6]

It has also been developed and shared by Nobel laureate Archbishop Desmond Tutu, who believes there can be no real ubuntu unless there is equality and integration in society. In the opinion of Professor Thaddeus Metz, who teaches Philosophy at the University of Johannesburg, "for many southern African intellectuals, communion and harmony consists of identifying with and exhibiting solidarity towards others, in other words, enjoying a sense of togetherness, cooperating and helping people – out of sympathy and for their own sake."[7]

Challenging Nigeria's Traditional Gender Roles: Ifeoma Idigbe[8]

I am reminded of the power of ubuntu every time I visit sub-Saharan Africa, most recently during that visit to Lagos, where I was so struck by the innovative ideas and transformative vision of the people I met, so much fresher and modern than many I meet in Europe.

I was attending a lunch with a group of fellows of WIMBIZ (Women in Management, Business & Public Service), an association to promote the development of female executives in different sectors of Nigerian society. Its past Chairman, Ifeoma Idigbe, is one of the founders of *boys to Men*, an NGO that helps disadvantaged young men find their way in business. Idigbe has worked in banking and finance, as an entrepreneur and in the public sector. She is the author of *Sounds of Silence: Musings*, a collection of 131 philosophical writings on life, inspired by the author's reflection on the meaning of things, and lessons learned from hers and others experiences.

During our conversation, she raised a number of ideas echoing issues facing other parts of the world. She started by telling me why they set up boys to Men: "Interacting with young people, I realized that there was an imbalance. When I talked to the girls, they seemed to be very clear about what they wanted to achieve and showed a strength of character. When I talked to the boys it would be a case of "we want to make money" but there was no clear statement about how.

> There was a pattern. More girls had a sense of where they were headed, and there are many women's organizations supporting women. In Nigeria, girls are brought up to be strong, because it's a male-oriented society. Girls are brought up in case they marry husbands who can't look after them, in case they marry husbands who are not nice to them, so they are able to look after themselves. For example, if a woman loses her job, she may be unhappy, but the next day she might start selling things, she might now find a trade, or start selling food or something just to generate income, she won't just sit back and wait. Women are increasingly getting stronger than men in terms of their ability to survive difficulty. And they don't have the same ego problems as men. I decided to set up the Boys to Men Foundation to talk about these issues and to run programs to try to change the mindset of boys and to teach them that they should not worry if their wives are the breadwinner. If she has a better job and she's given a house, then accept it. The important thing is to do well as a family. These are the mindset changes that I want to address."

Traditional gender roles in Nigeria are partly to do with religion in a country where 50% of the population is Muslim, 40% is Christian and the remainder adhere to local religions. To help professional women and entrepreneurs, 13 people—one man and 12 women including Idigbe—founded Women in Management Business and Public Service (WIMBIZ) at the beginning of the century: We were surprised by the success of the platform, and so we suddenly found ourselves introducing programs. Women needed a platform that would give them the courage to change their lives if they wanted to. Since then, the government has fostered some initiatives to increase the presence of women on boards.

"Sometimes I believe that the challenge is not about giving women opportunities in management, but about women themselves wanting those positions. In my experience, sometimes women don't want to be the managing director. They may want to be the executive director, but they don't necessarily want the final responsibility, because their lives are divided into various other compartments, and sometimes, women will leave their jobs because of their children to take some time for my children, and then go back to work. That affects their careers.

There is misogyny in the Nigerian business world that puts many women off. But I think that many are simply afraid of women and the changes that their presence will mean, changes to how things are done. Personally, I get on very well with men and have always been able to adapt to male-dominated situations. But I also think things are getting better, but very slowly. The World Economic Forum estimates it will take about a hundred years for women to achieve parity with men in the workplace. I'm not sure it will take that long, but I'm not sure either that it will be totally men's fault, it will be a combination of whether the women who are in positions at particular times want to continue in those positions."

If there is one continent where it's easy to see rapid change taking place, it's Africa. The youngest population on the planet, and arguably the most imaginative, it is integrating rapidly into global society and with fewer resources than other regions. This imagination and entrepreneurial drive could lead the continent to advance rapidly with policies of inclusion and diversity, more so than other regions with older populations more resistant to change. The presence of women in the private sector and in public life will doubtless contribute to this transformation. And the ubuntu philosophy may act as a catalyst for integration and inclusion.

Notes

1. Kwasi Wiredu (ed.), *A Companion to African Philosophy* (*Blackwell Companions to Philosophy*) (Oxford: Blackwell, 2004); Kindle ed.
2. Ibid., Kindle ed., loc. 228–229.
3. Ibid., Kindle ed., loc. 238.
4. N. Nzegwij, Feminism and Africa: Impact and Limits of the Metaphysics of Gender, in *A Companion to African Philosophy (Blackwell Companions to Philosophy)*, op. cit., Kindle ed., loc. 9265–9266.
5. Ibid., Kindle ed., loc. 9306.

6. T. Metz, What Archbishop Tutu's Ubuntu Credo Teaches the World About Justice and Harmony, *The Conversation*, October 4, 2017. http://theconversation.com/what-archbishop-tutus-ubuntu-credo-teaches-the-world-about-justice-and-harmony-84730.
7. Ibid.
8. The quotes in this section were extracted from an interview between Ifeoma Idigbe with the author on September 16, 2019.

Index

A

Abc 140
Adorno, Theodor 159
Aeschylum 95
Affirmative action 6, 11, 160
Africa 75, 81, 111, 147, 167–169, 171
AI (artificial intelligence) 19, 26, 31, 57–59, 100, 130, 131
Airbnb 99, 102
Alcázar Silvela, Diego del 64
Algorithms 57–60, 102, 130
Amazon 12, 57, 109, 146
Analytical philosophy 50, 51, 67, 68, 82
Anderson Cancer Center 49
Apartheid 83
Apel, K.O. 142
Aporofobia 140, 149
Aquinas, Thomas St. 51, 53, 81, 157
Argentina 91, 112
Aristotle 30, 41, 51, 53, 60, 76, 97, 143, 149
Australia 5, 114
Automation 130, 132, 148

B

Bain & Company 160
Beebee, Helen 5
Behringwerke AG 49
Bennett, Jessica 166
Bentham, Jeremy 85, 89
Berklee School of Music 125
Bible, The 157
Big data 57, 68, 117
Binghamton University 168
Blücher, Heinrich 111
Bouygues, Helen Lee 116, 117, 119
Boyatzis, Richard 69, 70
Brazil 47, 48, 107–109, 167
Brennan, Samantha 5
BRICS (Brazil, Russia, India, China, South Africa) 107, 118
British Airways 156
British Council 156
Brown, Gene 141
Business case 85, 86, 89, 144
Business ethics 76, 103, 140, 141, 143–145, 148
Butterfield, Stewart 98

C

Cambridge University 32, 46, 50, 59, 60, 82, 88, 89
Cameroon 169
Campos, Stella 118
Camus, Albert 127, 132, 159
Canada 5, 23, 111
Canetti, Elías 67
Cardinal Virtues 54
Cardoso, Ruth 109
Carnegie, Andrew 44
Carnegie, foundation 101
Castro, Fidel 162
Catalonia 83
Catalyst 78, 87, 171
Catholic 81, 139
Cave, allegory of the 55, 121
Channel 4 155
Chenavier, Robert 128
Chesky, Brian 99
Chile 91, 136
China 33–36, 45, 107, 109, 163, 164
Christianity 126, 127, 129, 131
Cicero 97, 159, 163, 165
Cleveland, Grover 51
CNN 103
Coca-Cola 28
Collins, Jim 46, 55, 60
Columbia University 94
Communism 37
Compassion 30, 42, 69–71, 73, 147
Conference Board, The 144, 149
Confucius 30, 37, 45
Conill, Jesús 140, 149
Conradi, Peter J. 67, 72
Contractualism 53, 60
Cooper, Gary 38
Criado Pérez, Caroline 17
CSR (Corporate Social Responsibility) 43, 85, 88, 143–145, 148
Cuadrivium 94
Cultural Revolution 33
Cyrus, Miley 125

D

Danos, Paul 115
Davos 61
Deming, David 99
Deontology 43, 53, 59, 84, 115, 148
Descartes, René 25, 30, 32, 81
Devlin, Lord 95, 96, 105
Diversity 1–3, 6, 11–14, 21, 36, 48, 69, 70, 79, 85–87, 89, 109, 115, 117, 118, 123, 143–147, 156, 159–161, 165, 168, 169, 171
Drucker, Peter 47, 50, 59, 110, 139, 148
Dualism 25, 30
Dummett, Michael 82
Dworkin, Gerald 140
Dworkin, Ronald 60

E

EFMD (European Foundation for Management Development) 1
Eichmann, Adolf 112–114, 117
El Comercio 136
El País 140
Emoticons 69
Engels, Friedrich 132
Enron 101, 117
Entrepreneurship 34, 61, 88, 98, 128, 146
Equatorial Guinea 169
Europe 20, 33, 48, 75, 78, 92, 97, 107, 111, 112, 140, 146, 147, 154, 164, 169
European Union 140, 143
Evans, Peter 153

F

Facebook 8, 13, 99
Feminism 5, 156–158, 161–163, 165, 171
Feminist philosophy 4, 5, 165, 168

Financial Times 117
Finn, Ed 57, 60
Fiorina, Carly 99
Ford, foundation 101
Fordism 129
France 76, 91, 127, 128, 158, 162, 164
Free market 6, 39
Friedman, Marilyn 6
Friedman, Milton 40, 46, 146, 149
Fuentes, Carlos 127
Fuhrmans, Vanessa 17
Fundação Getulio Vargas 107

G

Galt, John (fiction) 38
Gandhi, Indira 51
Gandhi, Mahatma 95
Gates, Bill 130
Geach, Mary 82, 88
Gebbia, Joe 99
Gekko, Gordon (fiction) 44
General Motors 146
Germany 33, 44, 49, 127
Ghoshal, Sumantra 100, 101, 145
Goldberg, Whoopi 122
Gramsci, Antonio 129
Green Carmichael, Sarah 17
Greenspan, Alan 39
Gross-Loh, Christine 35, 45
The Guardian 45, 58, 72, 132
Guevara, Che 162

H

Hare, R.M. 67
Harman, Gilbert 23, 31
Harris, Parker 99
Hart, H.L.A. 89, 105
Hartley, Scott 98, 105
Harvard 9, 10, 14, 37, 99

Hate 58, 95, 96, 147, 148
Hausner, Gideon 112
Hawking, Stephen 58, 130
Hegel, F. 126
Heidegger, Martin 111
Herbert, George 127
Hermes 34
Hewlett-Packard 99
Hill, Andrew 117, 119
Hobbes, Thomas 114, 119
Hoffman, Reid 99
Hollywood 14, 38, 56
Homer 24, 31, 131
Hopkins, Nancy 78, 87
Horkheimer, Max 159
Humanities 4, 7, 10, 11, 54, 62, 63, 65, 71, 77, 91–94, 97–99, 102–104, 112, 130, 147, 168
Hume, David 51, 52, 59
Humility 43, 55
Husserl, Edmund 111
Hutchison, Katrina 5, 6
Hypatia 5

I

IBM 2
IE Business School 1, 3, 20, 29, 123, 156, 160
IE University 3, 22, 29, 33, 45, 64, 107, 123
Inclusion 2, 3, 6, 11–15, 21, 33, 36, 64, 75, 78, 79, 108, 109, 123, 144, 147, 156, 159–161, 164, 165, 171
India 107, 167
Integrity 43, 80, 137
Invisible Women 17
Israel 39, 75
Italy 91, 93, 127
ITV 155

J

Jacobs Engineering 20
Japan 163, 164
Jarvis Thomson, Judith 31, 56, 60
Jaspers, Karl 111
Jenkins, Fiona 5, 17
Jiang Xuan Yi 34
Job 8, 10, 13, 48, 92, 94, 96, 97, 116, 128, 130, 136, 142, 152, 155, 156, 163, 164, 170, 171
Jobs, Steve 99
Johnson, Boris 151
Johnson & Johnson 63
Jurisprudence 4, 93, 95, 105

K

Kafka, F. 155
Kahnemann, Daniel 32
Kalanick, Travis 39
Kant, Immanuel 5, 17, 84, 110, 138, 148
Kenya 151, 152
Kettering Cancer Center 49
Keynes, John M. 50
Kotter, John P. 44, 46

L

Laissez-faire 40
Lebanon 75
Lewis, C.S. 82
LGBTQI 95, 123
LHH-DBM 136
Liberal democracy 6
Liberalism 96, 101
Libertarianism 37, 39, 40, 45
Lifelong learning 29, 31
LinkedIn 99
Liszt, Franz von 140
Locke, John 39
Lodish, Harvey 78, 87
Loughlin, Steve 99
Love 10, 16, 19, 34, 64, 68, 72, 94, 111, 122, 124
Luther King Jr., Martin 95

M

M&A (mergers and acquisitions) 135
Machiavelli, N. 81
Management 2, 3, 6–8, 15–17, 27–29, 36, 41, 44, 47, 49, 50, 54, 55, 58, 71, 72, 75–77, 80, 82, 94, 100–104, 109, 110, 115, 117, 131, 132, 135, 137, 139, 141–144, 148, 154, 159–161, 164, 169–171
Mandela, Nelson 95, 169
Mao Zedong 33, 162
Marshall, Stephen 67
Marx, Karl 125, 126, 128, 129, 131, 132
Marxism 126, 128
Mases, Jack 168
May of 68 112
MBA 1, 20, 65, 75, 76, 102, 108, 123, 135, 159–161, 166
McBride, William 158, 166
McCarthy, Joseph 112
McGill, Justine 6
McKinsey 17, 86, 89
MedDay 76
Medicare 39
Melatonin 29
Metaethics 51, 52
#Me Too 166
Metz, Thaddeus 169, 172
Mexico 62
Midgley, Mary 66
Migration 111
Milgram, Stanley 114–116
Mill, John Stewart 85, 89, 96, 105
Mintzberg, Henry 102, 105

MIT 11, 37, 60, 78, 79
Monism 25, 31
Montaigne, M. de 159, 162, 165
Moore, G.E. 51, 52, 59
Moral case 84, 144, 145
Morgan, J.P. 44, 146
Morgan Stanley 123
Musk, Elon 44, 58, 130

N

Nagel, Thomas 30, 32
Nazism 51, 66, 112, 115
NCVO (National Council for Voluntary Organizations) 153–155
Neal, Patricia 38
Nero 163
Neurophilosophy 4, 22, 23, 30
New Deal 39
New School for Social Research, The 112
The New Yorker 112
The New York Times 60, 88
New York University 136
NGO 153, 170
Nietzsche, Friedrich 41, 44, 45, 55, 145
Nigeria 167, 169, 170
Non-cognitivism 51, 52
Normative 51, 52, 100, 165
Novartis 20
Nzegwu, Nkiru 168

O

Objectivism 38–40, 46
The Observer 153
O'Connor, Frank 38
OECD 94, 108
O'Neill, Jim 107, 118
Orphazyme 76
Overlapping consensus 53

Ovid 19
Oxfam 154
Oxytocin 22, 27, 28

P

Parfitt, Derek 31
Pascoe, C.J. 123, 132
Paypal 99
Pearson 95, 104
Peikoff, Leonard 40–44, 46
PepsiCo 28
Peru 136, 138
Peter Drucker Forum 47
Peterson, Christopher 54, 60
Pinterest 99
Plato 4, 17, 26, 31, 32, 51, 53–55, 60, 67, 81, 87, 110, 121, 126, 128, 131, 132
Political liberalism 53
Pompeo, Mike 39
Populism 82
Princeton University 112
Principles 2, 7, 8, 25, 38, 40, 41, 50, 53, 59, 67, 76, 78, 80, 82, 84, 85, 87, 96, 99, 114, 125–128, 131, 138–140, 142–145, 148, 157, 161
Protestantism 131
Psychopharmacology 27–29
Puett, Michael 35, 45
Pythagoras 157

R

Rationality 34, 35, 43, 80, 142
Rawls, John 53, 60, 140
Reboot Foundation 116
Reich, Robert 37, 45
Reisman, George 39
Relate IQ 99
Renault 127–129

Republican Party 39
Rifkin, Jeremy 128
Roark, Howard (fiction) 38, 42
Roche 20, 21
Rockefeller, John D. 44
ROE (Return On Investment) 86
Rometty, Ginni 2
Roosevelt, F.D. 39
Rousseau, J.J. 81, 114, 119
Rules 12, 24, 36, 41, 53, 59, 68, 79, 84, 85, 87, 95, 102, 116, 117
Runnymede Trust 153
Russia 107
Ryan, Paul 39

S

Saint Augustine 111
Salesforce 99
Salk Institute 23
Sandberg, Sheryl 168
Sandford, Stella 159
Sarkozy, Nicolas 99, 100
Sartre, Jean Paul 128, 158, 159, 162, 166
Saul, Jennifer 5
Scandinavia 159, 160
Scanlon, Tim 53
Scarman, Lord 153
Schopenhauer, Arthur 5, 17
Scott, William Richard 100, 105
Seligman, Martin 54
Sen, Amartya 85, 89, 95
Seneca 159, 163, 165
Shanghai 34
Shang Xia 33–35
Silbermann, Ben 99
Silicon Valley 61
Slack 98
Smith, Robert Elliott 58
Socrates 4, 23, 80
Somerville College 51
Sontag, Susan 127
South Africa 83, 107, 169

South Summit 61–63
Spain 62–64, 83, 91, 112, 121, 127
Staël, Madame de 5
STEM (Science, Technology, Engineering and Mathematics) 11, 78, 79, 87, 96, 97
Stern, Günther 111
Stoic 163
Straub, Richard 47
Syria 75

T

Taylorism 110, 129, 132
Thatcher, Margaret 44, 51, 155
Thiel, Peter 99
Thomism 81
Thomson, David 121, 132
Trolley problem, the 55, 57, 60
Truman, Harry S. 81
Trump, Donald 37, 39, 60, 83
Tuck Business School 115
Turing, Alan 31
Turing Test 19, 31
Tutu, Desmond 169
Twitter 58, 69
Tyco 101

U

Ubuntu 169, 171
UK 152, 154, 156
United States (US) 1, 5, 20, 33, 37–39, 48, 78, 81, 83, 91, 97, 98, 109, 111, 112, 136, 140, 143, 144, 146, 147
University College London 20
University of British Columbia 22
University of California, Los Angeles 51
University of California, San Diego 22
University of Chicago 46, 95, 112
University of Dartmouth 115

University of Manitoba 23
University of Munich 140
University of Oxford 23, 99, 105
University of Sao Paulo 108, 109
University of South Florida 168
University of Valencia 140
Urbani Tartufi 93
US Business Roundtable 40
US Federal reserve 39
Utilitarianism 30, 43, 56, 84, 85, 89

Valiant, Virginia 5
Valor 118
Vasopressin 22, 27, 28
Vidor, King 38
Vienna 47
Vietnam War 39
Virtue ethics 53
Virtues 20, 30, 31, 42, 50, 53–55, 58–60, 94, 97, 147
Von Humboldt, Wilhelm 66, 97
Von Mises, Ludwig 39, 47

Wales, Jimmy 39, 155
Wall Street 18, 44
Warnock, Mary 17, 127, 132

Weber, Max 88, 132, 133, 141, 142, 145, 148, 149
West Point 8, 41
Wikipedia 39
Williams, Bernard 58, 60
WIMBIZ 169, 170
Wiredu, Kwari 168, 171
Wittgenstein, Ludwig 51, 81, 82, 88
Wojcicki, Susan 99
Wolfenden Report 95, 105
Wollstonecraft, Mary 5
World War II 51, 81, 111, 113

Xanthippe 4, 17
Xing Tonghe 34

Yahve 24
Yale University 114, 118, 166
Youtube 99, 136

Zakaria, Fareed 103
Zeno of Elea 55
Zuckerberg, Mark 44, 99
Zweig, Stefan 71, 73

GPSR Compliance

The European Union's (EU) General Product Safety Regulation (GPSR) is a set of rules that requires consumer products to be safe and our obligations to ensure this.

If you have any concerns about our products, you can contact us on

ProductSafety@springernature.com

In case Publisher is established outside the EU, the EU authorized representative is:

Springer Nature Customer Service Center GmbH
Europaplatz 3
69115 Heidelberg, Germany

www.ingramcontent.com/pod-product-compliance
Lightning Source LLC
LaVergne TN
LVHW010341260326
834688LV00036B/827